# Cross-Country Skiing . . .
# The Natural Way

# Cross-Country Skiing . . . The Natural Way

## Leif Odmark

with Pat Thornton

Contemporary Books, Inc.
Chicago

**Library of Congress Cataloging in Publication Data**

Odmark, Leif.
    Cross-country skiing . . . the natural way.

    Includes index.
    1. Cross-country skiing.    I. Thornton, Pat, joint
author.    II. Title.
GV854.9.C7035    1978        796.9'3        77-23702
ISBN 0-8092-7798-0
ISBN 0-8092-7797-2 pbk.

Published by Contemporary Books, Inc.
180 North Michigan Avenue, Chicago, Illinois 60601
Manufactured in the United States of America
Library of Congress Catalog Card Number: 77-23702
International Standard Book Number: 0-8092-7798-0 (cloth)
                                    0-8092-7797-2 (paper)

Published simultaneously in Canada by
Beaverbooks
953 Dillingham Road
Pickering, Ontario L1W 1Z7
Canada

# Contents

# Acknowledgments

Drawings by Sherry Fowler

Photos by Norris Clark, Sherry Fowler, Bob Lee, Joe Leonard, Fred Lindholm, Ann Puchner, Morgan Renard, Don Rosebrock, GoGo Schwartz, Sun Valley News Bureau, Dick Wiethorn, and *Wood River Journal*

Special thanks to Shannon Besoyan, Judy Bockman, Armand S. Deutsch, Corby Dibble, Suzi Gillis, Jean Lane, JoAnn Levy, Dr. Lynn "Buck" Levy, Lois Meyer, Richard Meyer, Herman Primus, Barbara Reidy, Sawtooth Helicopters Inc., and Gun Taylor

Cover photograph by Sun Valley News Bureau

# Introduction

In a sport in which everyone who has done it more than once suddenly becomes a self-styled expert, Leif Odmark is uniquely qualified to write a book about cross-country skiing. He grew up on skis, literally putting on his first pair about the time he learned to walk in his native Järved, Örnsköldsvik, Sweden.

"I can remember strapping a lunch on my back and skiing the 13 miles to school," he said. "At that time, cross-country skiing, to me, was not a sport or fun, it was transportation."

Later, cross-country skiing took on new emphasis and did become both a sport as well as fun for Odmark. He excelled in the sport that, for Swedes, is a way of life and became a member of the Swedish National Team for cross-country racing.

He also excelled at soccer and was recognized as one of the country's leading players. In 1948 the Swedish Viking Club of Chicago picked up the entire tab to bring Odmark to the United States to become a member of the club-sponsored soccer team.

Later, he made his way by bus to Sun Valley, Idaho. He got as far as Twin Falls, Idaho, before being stopped by a snow-storm. Everything was at a standstill when word came that an old caretaker was stranded in the mountains. Odmark set out on his cross-country skis and rescued the man.

Once he had arrived at Sun Valley, it did not take the young Swede long to establish himself as one of the top instructors in the resort's alpine ski school.

In addition, he later directed his own alpine ski school at Coronet Peak, South Island, New Zealand; was director of the swimming and diving school at Balboa Bay Club, Newport Beach, California; and headed his own swimming program at Sun Valley. He played ice hockey with a championship team, and still, from time to time, enjoys playing golf and tennis.

In 1952 Leif Odmark was head coach for the U. S. Nordic Olympic Team that competed in the classic combined and spe-cial cross-country events at Oslo, Norway. He is still a certi-fied alpine ski instructor, helped set up standards and wrote the examination manual for certification of Nordic instructors, and serves as chairman of the Northern Intermountain Profes-sional Ski Instructors Association (NIPSIA), Nordic Division.

Scott USA, a ski-equipment manufacturer, recognized Od-mark's expertise and unique knowledge of the fundamentals of cross-country skiing and sought him out to help design Nordic ski poles. The company subsequently sent him to the Winter Olympics at Sapporo, Japan, where the poles were successfully tested by the world's leading cross-country ski rac-ers.

Despite his background and proficiency in so many diversi-fied sports, Odmark's interest in cross-country skiing in gen-eral, and touring in particular, never diminished. In the win-ter of 1971-1972, he opened his own Sun Valley Nordic Ski School and Touring Center, one of the first such schools in the country.

"I have been teaching sports for a long, long time," he said, "and I thought it was about time people learned the proper way to enjoy cross-country skiing."

"I think it is very important with every sport that people learn the right way from the beginning. Of course I realize not everyone can come to Sun Valley to take lessons, and that is the reason I have agreed to write this book—so you can learn the right way to cross-country ski and enjoy the sport as much as I do."

Leif Odmark getting ready for a cross-country ski lesson with one of his students—Jackie Onassis.

# Cross-Country Skiing . . .
# The Natural Way

# 1
# History

I grew up in Järved, Örnsköldsvik, Sweden, where it seemed that cross-country skis were a normal extension to my own feet. The skis were my means of transportation and I, like the others who lived in the area, relied upon them to go everywhere during the winters.

For that reason, I never really gave too much thought to how cross-country skis came into being or who invented them. The skis were just always there—and have been for thousands of years, I have come to learn.

But who actually was the first to develop skiing is still a big question. The Norwegians say they were the first to use skis. The Finns say they were. And, of course, the Russians claim it, too.

But I like to think it was the Swedes, mostly because there is some pretty strong archaeological evidence to back up my claim. The remains of primitive skis were found above Sweden's Arctic Circle. These have been carbon-dated to 2000 B.C.

Also some prehistoric cave drawings were found above the Arctic Circle, and they indicate that the human inhabitants of

This pair of skis was hewed by hand years ago out of two small trees found in the Stanley Basin mountains.

the area may have used skis made from the long bones of animals. There is also some indication that hunters wore one long ski for support and a short ski covered with fur to push themselves across the snow.

Legends, of course, provide further "evidence." I think we can safely call legends evidence of a sort because they grew out of something, even if it was just someone's imagination.

Because of my Scandinavian heritage, I am proud, too, to claim one of the Norwegians' favorite legends that says Norway's soldiers of the Middle Ages patrolled on skis and were able to carry Prince Haakon over the deep snow to safety from enemies of the crown. There is a famous painting, done in 1206, of the event and it shows the Birkebeiners, or soldiers, wearing skis.

Nobody today knows exactly how far Prince Haakon was carried, but there is an annual cross-country ski race in Norway that commemorates saving him. It is named the Birke-beiner Lopet, in honor of the soldiers, and covers 40 miles.

We Swedes have our own commemorative race, too—the Va-saloppet (Vasa, for short), which some have called "the most excruciating ski race known to man." I can readily testify that it is, indeed, a very difficult race.

That race, too, is based on a legend. It is said that Gustav Vasa fled the town of Mora on skis after unsuccessfully trying to persuade the Swedes to revolt against the Danes. He reached Salen, 53 miles away, and was caught there by a group of young Swedes from Mora, who had been persuaded by wiser elders that the revolt was in order. Vasa was convinced the Swedes were sincere so he lead a successful rebellion, which, in turn, resulted in his becoming King Gustav I.

The first Vasaloppet was in 1922 and there were 119 entries, mostly local boys. Fifty-five years later, in 1977, 11,527 people, most of whom were international competitors, competed in the 53-mile race. Super skier Ivan Garanin became the first

Thousands of cross-country ski racers in a mass start of a race in Switzerland.

Soviet to win this, the Grand Prix of cross-country ski races, as he lead the field in completing the course in four hours, thirty minutes.

The big hero of the 1977 Vasa, however (at least for the Swedes), was Carl XVI Gustav, who became the second Swedish king to travel the course on cross-country skis. Only two or three race officials knew ahead of time about his secret start, but word got around quickly, and soon the 25,000 spectators were cheering loudly as the king beat more that 5,000 other racers to the finish. His majesty said later that he had practiced in the French countryside, covering 250 miles in preparing himself for the big challenge. He finished number 5,708 in a time of eight hours, twelve minutes, thus beating more than half of the contestants. When it was all over, Carl XVI Gustav even admitted, "It was great fun!"

King Karl XVI
Gustav of Sweden

That's really something to say that racing 55 miles on cross-country skis is "great fun"!

But enough of the present and back to the history. For most Scandinavians, cross-country skis remained something strictly functional until the mid-nineteenth century when recreation was introduced. The first known cross-crountry ski race was held in northern Norway in 1843. The first Holmenkollen jumping and skiing event, one of the biggest winter happenings in Europe today, was on the outskirts of Oslo in 1892.

Swedish and other Scandinavian immigrants are credited with introducing cross-country skis to the United States before the Civil War. It was many years later that Norwegian-born Jon Torsteinson became the only link during winter between mining camps in Nevada and civilization in California. He became something of a folk hero and was known as John "Snowshoe" Thompson. What he did for 20 years was carry the mail over the Sierra Mountains from Placerville, California, to Carson City, Nevada, on skis he made himself. It took him three days to make the trip.

These Scandinavians are really something!

Since the time of "Snowshoe" Thompson, interest in cross-country skiing, and touring in particular, has become more and more popular. In 1971, the *Wall Street Journal* reported that cross-country skiing was the fastest-growing sport in the world. That year, 50,000 pairs of skis were imported into the United States; and in two years, that number had tripled.

So you can see, cross-country skiing is something more than a fad, a passing fancy. It is a method of winter transportation that permits you to see all of those wonderful and beautiful places you hiked and backpacked to during the summer.

But if you are not a hiker or a backpacker and prefer to limit yourself to something a little less strenuous, you may wish to enjoy yourself touring the golf course or backyard.

Either way, cross-country skiing is healthy. And if you can walk, you can cross-country ski. If you do it right.

So now is the time to start doing it right. Welcome to the new world of winter enjoyment.

# 2
# Conditioning

Cross-country skiing is not only an enjoyable recreation but also an excellent all-around conditioner that can contribute to your general health and fitness in many ways.

When you are cross-country skiing, all of your body's major muscle groups—in arms, legs, back, abdomen, chest—are active. It is this activity that contributes to your overall physical fitness.

I should say right here and now that when I say overall physical fitness, I do not mean bulging muscles. Throughout my many years of skiing with world class cross-country skiers, I have not met one man who looks like Mr. Atlas nor one woman who resembles a Russian shot-putter. On the contrary, people who cross-country ski are generally well-proportioned, slim, and lithe. They are truly beautiful people, both physically and mentally, because being out-of-doors and exercising is good for the mind and body.

We hear a lot these days about aerobic activity that directly benefits the heart and the lungs. Cross-country skiing is one of the very best of the aerobics. And, as in other forms of physical activity, as you ski more and more, you will note that you are progressively less and less tired after a day of cross-country. This is one of the biggest benefits and one of the surest signs of improving and increasing physical fitness.

Of course, everyone who will be taking up cross-country skiing should want to prepare himself or herself so as to enjoy the sport more and keep from becoming too tired. I am not talking about racers who train the year around but about people who want to learn to cross-country ski so they can just glide around on top of the snow, meandering through nature. This is the cross-country ski tourer—the person for whom this book is written.

There are many different ways to condition yourself for skiing. Students at my Sun Valley Nordic Ski School often ask for suggestions, and I always tell them I think it is a good idea to start *at your own tempo, your own speed.* You will be hearing that phrase throughout this book, so you might as well start out adjusting to yourself, and not to somebody else's longer or shorter legs or bigger or smaller lung capacity.

Throughout the country, there are health clubs and athletic associations at which you can get into a program designed for physical development. The national YMCA has an excellent physical fitness program that would be a great primer for cross-country skiing.

For that reason (and the fact that I don't know exactly what your physical condition is at the moment) I am not going to give you specific exercises, one, two, three; but, rather, I will make suggestions on which you can develop your own method of conditioning. For example, on your own, you can begin jumping rope, which is a tremendous conditioner. It builds not only the legs but the arms, the lungs, and the heart as well.

Another suggestion is to take the dog for a walk . . . even if you don't have a dog. Walk instead of taking the bus, or if you must ride, get off a stop or two early and walk the rest of the way. Bypass the elevator in favor of the stairs, or at least catch the elevator higher than ground level. Hiking, too, is

Leif Odmark (dark sweater) leads members of the U.S. Olympic cross-country team during training at Sun Valley, Idaho, in 1952. Joining Leif in chasing antelope are (from left): John Burton; John Caldwell, who later became a U.S. Olympic coach; Si Dunklee; and George Howland.

Running with cross-country ski poles is one form of conditioning on dry land for a season of racing.

very good. Bicycling is excellent, of course. Utilize your parks for jogging. Go out and play ball with the kids.

Anything you can do to condition your body will be good for you and help your cross-country skiing. Swimming is a very good conditioner for the entire body. Do calisthenics: Raise up on your toes, stretch, then go down into knee bends. Raise your arms and twist. Sit in a chair and do a swimming crawl kick. This is great for the leg muscles. Install a "hanging bar" then grab and hang and stretch. Run in place, at different speeds. Extend your arms and twist, turn, and bend. Lie on the floor and lift a small weight, a child works well, with your legs. Sit on the floor and, with knees raised, "run" or "walk" with your feet.

Let me caution you, though, not to overdo. Regular short exercises that you like and enjoy doing several times a week are far better than strenuous workouts that you avoid.

Cross-country ski racers begin conditioning and training on dry land.

So take it easy while you become more flexible and limber. Strengthen your body and wind capacity. And do it at your own tempo, at your own speed. Make it fun. You should never train in such a way that you despise it. You should do what is right for you. You should actually set up a program suitable to yourself and your work schedule, be it in an office, at home, or on a physical job. Bring yourself into condition so you can enjoy cross-country skiing. Set a goal and check your own progress.

A very important part of conditioning, of course, is lung capacity. Once you have that, your mind and your head will be much more clear. From there on, you can go into specialized exercises for certain parts of the body that may need additional help.

What I want to stress about conditioning, though, is that people should prepare themselves physically so they can enjoy skiing more. All the time I see people come to Sun Valley to learn to cross-country ski, but, instead, it takes them four days just to get into shape.

So let's get healthy now and stay that way the year around. Have a program set up that lends itself to fitness 12 months of the year. If you stay in shape, everything you like to do is going to come a lot easier, especially cross-country skiing.

# 3
# The Basics

A great advantage of cross-country skiing is that it is not necessary to travel to a mountain resort in order to enjoy the sport.

You can cross-country ski anywhere there is a depth of a couple inches of snow on a grass base. If you happen to have enough snow in your own backyard, that would be an ideal place to start. Especially if you are a little shy or unsure of yourself, the backyard has the advantage of offering privacy. Besides, this book would be right at your fingertips.

If you have more self-confidence, you may wish to start out in a bigger space, such as a golf course, a park or on a little country road that has a soft—but not gravel—base. None of these places requires much snow at all. You can cross-country ski on just a few inches snow base. That may surprise you because we are always hearing the Alpine ski resorts brag about the tremendous snow depths they have on their mountains.

On a golf course, for example, if you have a three or four inch base of snow, you can glide along smoothly and you

11

don't have to worry about hurting the bottoms of your skis. If you come to a paved road or a gravel road, you may wish to take your skis off and carry them across, then put them back on when you are on the other side. Cross-country skis are so easy to put on and take off that crossing a road in this manner hardly slows you down at all.

However, if you have nonwax skis and prefer not to take them off, you can cross the road by stepping without gliding—what I would call a light walk. In other words, lift your ski straight up and set it back straight down, without sliding your skis at all. If you are careful and walk lightly in this manner, you will not hurt the base of your skis.

On the other hand, if you have a ski that is waxed, you must take it off. Otherwise, you will have a fine collection of rocks and gravel attached to the waxy base.

There are different kinds of snow, and each affects skiing. Even when you become proficient in your cross-country skiing, the condition of the snow will determine how far and how fast you will move on your skis.

Snow conditions are discussed more thoroughly in connection with waxing, but for now, let me give you an example of what I mean: If you have cold snow, called powder snow, you will find it a little more difficult to get much of a glide, especially when you are not using a prepared Nordic track. In these conditions, you will probably find yourself sinking down through the snow, so you will have to work a little harder and you won't glide as much.

In the spring, there is a phenomenon called corn snow. It is warmer and more solid and has a little crust on top. You can stay on top of corn or warm snow so naturally you will go a lot farther and faster, and skiing will be a lot easier for you.

When you are touring with a party, no matter what the snow conditions are, it is a good idea to take turns breaking track. If the snow is deep or has a breakable crust, one person should go first, leading the group for 50 or 60 yards, then step to the side and go last; the next person takes over the lead for 50 or 60 yards, and so forth. No one will become overly tired,

Switch leads frequently when touring.

and you will have developed a very nice track for your return.

In addition, breaking track will give you a very good experience in learning how it feels to go through deep snow without seeing your skis. It is very important that you do not panic when your skis sink into the snow out of sight.

You may find at first that your skis feel a little wobbly when you don't have a solid base on which to stand. The natural thing to do is to hang on by curling your toes. Many times, our natural instincts are right, but in this case it is something you should not do. Concentrate on relaxing your toes. Stretch your toes out flat and keep them relaxed. After a while the skiing will come easier and you won't have to worry about it.

If possible, it is a good idea to develop your skiing both on and off soft snow. This change is especially good for your balance. You will see the difference when you go back to a packed slope or a good, well-established trail. Suddenly you will find skiing a lot easier.

You will need skis with bindings, poles, and cross-country

ski boots. I recommend nonwax skis to start. You need to have knowledge and the basic skills before you tackle waxing.

Take advantage of the rental equipment at a nearby Nordic ski center and rent your first skis. Later, if you want to buy your own skis, many shops and touring centers that rent equipment will deduct the cost of rental from the sale price.

You do not need to buy special clothing to cross-country ski, nor do you need clothing that is waterproof. When dressing for cross-country skiing, do not select a quilted or other heavy parka or jacket. Rather, you should wear many layers of things that you can peel off as you get warm. For example, choose a turtleneck, a shirt, and a thin windbreaker that you can take off and tie around your waist.

When you start out, you can use your blue jeans if you want to. In fact, this style is very popular. Girls, in particular, buy long, colorful kneesocks and put them over the blue jeans. This style is called "knicker blues." Knickers, of course, are ideal, and you will probably want to include them in your cross-country wardrobe eventually because they allow freedom of stride, are handier, and are more comfortable for skiing.

So, there you are. The bare essentials you will need to start cross-country skiing are this book, three or four inches minimum of snow base, rented nonwax skis with bindings, boots, poles, and whatever lightweight layers of clothes you happen to have already in your closet.

# 4
# The First Step

The best possible way to learn to cross-country ski is to take some lessons from a good, certified touring school. But be sure you learn from a certified instructor. In case you are not near a school, this book is designed to help you get started off on the right foot. If you are able to go to a certified school, this book will be very helpful in reviewing what you have learned.

To begin, there is a left ski and a right ski, and there *is* a difference. However, that difference lies only in the bindings. The skis, themselves, are the same, or should be. The serial numbers should match.

Both skis should have the same camber. Fiberglass skis have the best matching camber. If you happen to get wooden skis, which are becoming harder to find these days, look over the camber carefully to be sure both skis match. If they do not, pick out another pair.

Cross-country bindings are made to fit the shape of the boot, and the inside of the bindings should be marked either with a stamped "left" and "right" or have an outline of a foot indicating left and right.

Nordic boots. Almost all of the cross-country ski boots on the market today have what is known as the Nordic "norm fit" standardized sole. All four of these boots will fit the same pin binding.

Boots today are made in what is called a standard or Nordic "norm fit." This is one of the best improvements made in the industry since the beginning of mass-produced skis. What norm fit means is that your medium-sized standard left and right bindings will properly fit your left and right cross-country ski boot, no matter whether it is a size 5 or a size 13 or a size in between. Probably about 99 percent of the standard adult cross-country boots sold today have the same bottoms, and all of the bindings are the same standard size. And this is beautiful!

Before the norm fit standard was adopted by the industry, you had a different size binding for different size shoe widths and nothing ever really fit properly. You had to file down or shim up or make other alterations. Nothing was interchangeable.

Also, if you are an Alpine skier, you know that without norm fit, you have to take your skis in to a shop or to an expert to have the bindings adjusted. If someone borrows your skis, everything has to be reset. But because of norm fit, cross-country bindings do not require that adjustment, and you can loan your skis without worry about resetting bindings.

Looking at the bindings, you may wonder what keeps your boot in place. Turn your boot upside down and you will see three little holes in a row across the toe. These fit over the three little knobs on the base of the bindings that are called "pin bindings."

When you are ready to start skiing, you step into your skis, fit the holes in your boot over the knobs on the binding to hold the boot in place, and then press down the toe clamp to secure the bindings.

Take just a minute to look at that wire toe clamp. That is where these bindings get their second name, "mousetrap" bindings, because the wire springs up and down something like an old-fashioned mousetrap.

For regular cross-country skiing, which is done on rolling hills and on flat land, the pin, or mousetrap, bindings are the most popular and the easiest for the beginner. If you go into a

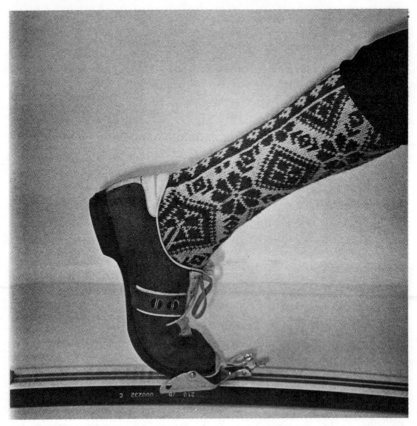

A three-pin, pole-operated binding gives the ski tourer the necessary freedom of the heel action.

little heavier touring, like over mountainous terrain, you will use a different style of binding that consists of a toe plate and a cable-type clamp. You also will be using a heavier boot. This binding looks somewhat similar to the old Alpine equipment that you hooked down for downhill skiing and unhooked for touring.

Mountaineering skis are not as wide as the old Alpine skis, but they are wider than the regular touring skis. Some also have steel edges, which you do not need in standard touring skis.

Now that you know all about bindings, the first thing to do is determine the difference between the left ski and the right, then lay them both down flat in the snow. Wipe the snow off the bottom of your boot and be sure the pin holes are clear of snow. Also wipe the snow from the pins. Place the toe of the boot over the pins. Secure the wire toe clamp over the top of the boot sole at the toe.

Your skis are now secured to your boot. Now is the time to pick up your poles. Many people make the mistake of grabbing the poles and holding them wrong. The poles are covered in depth in Chapter 6, but in the meantime, let me explain some basic rules.

There is a correct way to handle your poles. Notice the strap loop on the pole. This loop is adjustable. Place your hand

Grip. With the strap loop over the back of the hand, close your fingers around the pole handle catching the strap in your palm. Then plant the pole in the snow.

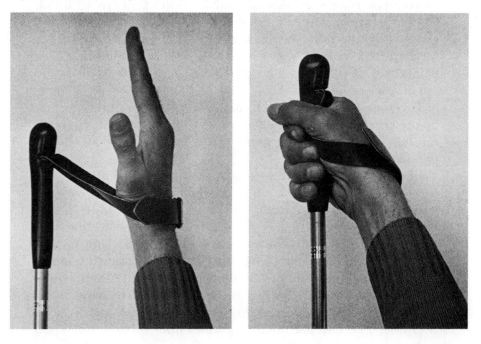

under the loop, then reach up through it. With your whole hand open, palm toward the pole, thumb up, let the loop fall to your wrist. Close your hand around the pole and the strap.

The strap will serve two purposes: It will prevent your hand from slipping down the pole too far and it will eliminate the need to grip the pole too hard. When skiing, your hand should be very relaxed.

Always adjust the length of the strap so your hand will not slip below the handle of the pole when you open your grip. Remember, when you push with the pole, you don't have to hang on hard to the pole; let the strap do the holding. Later, as you become more proficient at your skiing, your hand will be almost wide open, actually releasing your hold on the pole. It is the strap that will bring the pole back into your hand when you are ready.

You should understand the correct way to handle your poles from the beginning so you don't get into any bad habits.

Now you have your skis on and the poles properly in hand. The first thing you should do is to stand on one ski and gently slide the other ski back and forth across the snow. This forward-back motion will give you the feeling of gliding. For balance, it is perfectly all right to support yourself with the aid of your poles.

Those of you who are Alpine skiers may be startled at first by the sensation of the freedom of the heel. It will lift right up off the ski—and that is good. That is exactly what should happen.

Now, put most of your weight, about 90 percent of it, on the left ski and slide the right ski forward and back, forward and back. Allow your right heel to come up naturally in the back. The heel raising off the ski is exactly the feeling you want. Keep the ski on the snow and slide it back and forth a few times. Do the same thing with the left ski; putting about 90 percent of your weight on the right ski, slide the left one back and forth gently, letting the heel come up freely in back.

It is just exactly like walking. When you take a step, your heel does not stay flat on the ground, does it? Of course not.

When you first put on your skis, test the freedom of your heel. Particularly if you are already an alpine skier, the feeling of the heel lifting will be strange to you. Do this little exercise: Stand with your weight on one ski, then slide the other forward and back, letting the heel of the moving ski work freely.

Well, the same thing is true when you walk and glide on cross-country skis. The skis are just an extension of your toes, and your heel works just like it always does.

Also notice that when you walk, your knees bend slightly with each step. That slight bending is called a "soft knee." A soft knee is very important in cross-country skiing. You must not only remember to bend the knee, but also to concentrate on it. *Always ski with a soft knee!*

Now, let us take a walk. Just a walk, slowly and easily. I have already said cross-country skiing is very similar to walking. This will prove it. Walk on the skis, one step at a time. Do not actually pick the skis up out of the snow, though; let your heel rise in a natural way and just slide the skis along. Keep walking on them, shift your weight from foot-to-foot as you walk. This is just a normal, natural stride, except there are skis attached to your feet.

Always ski with a soft knee.

Don't worry about the glide at first, just keep walking. There should be a complete transfer of weight from ski to ski. It should be an exaggerated, severe step-over from ski to ski. All of your weight, the entire body weight shifts from left to right, right to left. Step out, lift your heel. Don't worry about not having much of a heel lift at first, it will come as you develop.

At first it may all feel very unnatural, so you will probably take small steps, a little shuffle-like motion and, as the result, your heel will not be raising much at all. But that's all right. When you become more accustomed to your skis, feel more comfortable, and have your balance, you will lengthen your stride and start transferring your weight more. That is when your heel will come up by itself. It is an automatic, natural thing.

Also, don't worry about the poles at this point. And do not be embarrassed if you reach out and catch yourself or tend to lean on them, using them as a crutch to help with your balance. That is a normal thing to do, and one that you will get away from as you become more accomplished.

Remember, the skis should be kept on the snow at all times during this short walk, so your action should be a gliding motion. Glide the ski. Slide one then the other along the snow. Get used to them; get to know the feeling of them moving across the snow.

Here is a little exercise that will be helpful at this point: Stand straight. Put all of your weight on the left ski, bend your right knee and pick up your right ski. Notice where the tip of your right ski is? That's right, it is still on the snow. You have to raise it specially by raising your toes. This effectively demonstrates what the loose heel is all about. Wiggle the ski back and forth a little and you will get the feeling of just how free and loose the heel is. But do you also notice how much support you have? Everything is very soft, very flexible, yet supportive.

Do the same thing with the left ski. Pick it up first by just bending the knee, then raise the tip with the toes. Wiggle the ski. Get the feeling of where the skis are and what you have to do to change a little direction. That is the important lesson in this exercise.

Another helpful exercise you can do at this point is to move around in a circle with the tips of the skis pointed toward the center. It is an easy maneuver besides being an excellent familiarization exercise. With your weight on the left ski, pick up the right one by lifting the heel. Move it to the right a little, then put the ski down again. Do the same thing with the left ski, bringing it back alongside the right one. Repeat until you have made a full circle pivoting around the toe.

Now go around the circle again, this time picking up the ski by lifting the toe, pivoting around the heel.

Repeat both of these exercises in the opposite direction.

An excellent warm-up exercise anytime you go skiing is to move your right ski forward, then bend down on your left knee. Your left heel will come up freely and automatically off the ski. You can use your poles for support for this exercise. Let your heel move up and down with the opposite knee forward. Bounce up and down to keep the knees soft. I call this a regular knee-bend warm-up, and I do it myself almost every time just before starting to ski.

You are now all loosened up and acquainted with the two important techniques—a soft knee and a loose heel. Now look around and pick out a spot. It could be a tree, a little knoll, or a rock. Anything will do as long as it is not too far away. Now gently and easily glide to it. Use the same walking and sliding you did on your first walk. If there is a little ski track there already that you can follow, do it. Following in one's footsteps, so to speak (having the skis in a set track) is always easier while learning. The track will aid you in staying in a straight line, keeping the skis parallel and from sliding sideways.

Ski in your own fashion, letting the heel come up and keeping your knees soft. Shift your weight. Don't worry about the poles yet, just slide the skis along to get the feeling of the glide. Transfer the weight.

Be sure to keep the knees soft. Concentrate on skiing with a bent-forward knee. Think about that as you are bending and softening that knee. You may have the feeling of sneaking around the track like a cat through the brush. This, by the way, is a very good exercise to build your strength.

It is very important to look ahead as you ski. Do not watch your feet. If you lose your balance, most of the time it is because your knees are too stiff and you are looking straight down at your feet.

The first few times out, just as with any new thing, you are probably fascinated by your skis and look at them. But it is very tiresome to ski looking down at the skis. Doing that is a mistake a lot of people make. So instead of looking at your skis, force yourself to look about one ski length ahead. After a while, when you have become comfortable on your skis, you can look around and enjoy the environment. And you will never miss watching the skis slide over and through the snow.

Let me emphasize again: Ski with a soft knee. Anytime you step from ski to ski, be sure to have a very soft knee. Point that knee. Lift the heel freely. And look one or more ski lengths ahead.

Practice these things now for a while. Become familiar with them before going on.

# 5
# Stepping Out

You have come a long way and probably admit to feeling fairly comfortable in gliding with a soft knee, shifting your weight, and looking at least one ski length ahead. So now it is time that we get you into what we call "the kick."

The kick does two things: (1) It pushes you forward; and (2) in doing so, the camber of your ski goes down to grip the snow.

The kick comes from the ball of the foot, and is probably best described as a push-off. The kick is what we refer to as a two-legged motion—the knee is in a strong, forward pressing position. Your left knee, for example, should be in that forward, pointed position. Now, step on the right ski, plant yourself, and push off.

Now you understand why I said the kick is a combination of a two-legged motion. A one, two. Establish a platform on your ski by stepping down with all of your weight on the right ski and push the left one. With the left knee in the forward drive position, you have a good glide. The heel releases and comes up in back on the right ski. As your weight automatically transfers to the left, repeat by pushing with your right ski.

The push is similar to the push-off used in ice skating. The emphasis is on the opposite leg—a strong, forward motion simultaneous with a pointed knee. That is where the heel has to come up.

Of course the first few times you try this motion, the skis will still be on the snow, but the heel of the boot will come up freely. And, you probably will not go too far with your first kick. In fact, the first time you try the kick, be very happy to see yourself go a couple inches. The kick may be difficult to do at first, because you will be going from one ski to the other, trying to balance on one foot at a time. You may be shaky, but this is nothing to be embarrassed about. We will be working on balance very soon.

So, if you get a couple of inches with the left push-off, then a couple more inches with the right push-off, you will have accomplished the forward motion and you should be very happy about it.

You have to keep in mind that you are moving on one ski at a time and it is very important to have that knee very soft. Remember that soft knee and also the importance of looking ahead approximately one ski length for balance.

Okay, let me say that all again: You should have a forward, pointed knee, the heel down, and look ahead for balance. The push-off leg is behind. Now transfer your weight to the forward leg and push off at the same time with the rear leg. Remember, the knee should be pointed. If you concentrate on this to begin with, it will become second nature and you will do very well as a cross-country skier.

A technique that is a very important part of Nordic skiing that you should be aware of is called "the diagonal." As you might guess from its name, the diagonal is simply alternate stride. It may sound confusing at this point, and I mention it now only because I want you to be aware of it, but I won't discuss it until we get to Chapter 6.

Now, let's go into the glide. We've already discussed how to do it, so it is time to talk about it in connection with developing it into a rhythm.

Let me say right away that you will never be able to develop a rhythm while you are hanging on to your poles. You don't need them as a crutch anymore. Besides, for this stage of your skiing, the poles are too awkward, too long, too much to handle. So lay them down out of the way; forget about them for the time being. That's right, you are going to ski without poles for a while.

Skiing without poles.

If you look at any beginning skiers, whether Alpine or Nordic, you are probably going to see them using their poles for balance. They put the poles out in front to hold themselves up. Let me explain why that is wrong: Most of the time when the pole is in front, it is going to fight the forward motion. Therefore, the pole should be held at a certain angle, which I will describe later.

Besides, the crutch is there, too, and it is tempting to use the poles in that manner. So by laying the poles down, you bypass the temptation to use them as crutches and to prevent them from stopping your forward motion.

I can assure you that once you have learned how to ski without poles, you don't miss them at all. Without them, you learn a natural balance and, of course, by having a natural balance, it is a lot easier to apply the poles to the motion you should have to help your forward motion, not to hinder it.

Without your poles, you are going to take a little walk, making use of the little track you made a few minutes ago on your first walk. When you go, try to remember all of those things you did when you had poles in hand: Bend your knees, keep them soft. Look ahead for balance. Shift your weight.

But before you actually step out, try to develop a little motion, a little rhythm of your own. To do that, stand still on both skis, swing your arms back and forth, forward then back past your hips like a pendulum. Bounce slightly on your flexible knees while you are doing it. This will help to remind you that your knees should be soft and flexible at all times.

This is a very simple motion, and exactly the same one you employ when you are walking or hiking. Try to do this standing still, then try to do the same thing when you are gliding. Bend your knees a little bit and shift your weight from ski to ski and ski swinging your arms back and forth.

I often wish I had music on the beginners' course at my Sun Valley Nordic Ski School in order that the students could bounce and swing their arms in time to the beat. Those who have a little more musical rhythm will pick up this rhythm a little easier.

Keeping your arms hanging loose, very loose, swing them sideways or forward and back, whatever you want to do. Don't you feel a little rhythm? Pretty soon your arms are going to fall into place as they should. It is a very natural thing. The opposite arm and leg move forward and back together, just the same as when you walk on dry land. The only difference is that in walking, you take a shorter stride; you don't have any glide involved. You step from here to there and don't glide any farther, as you do on skis.

So in skiing, you extend your step and arm motion a little more and you have a glide. That's all. It is that simple. Extend the walking motion into a gliding motion. The forward motion and the tempo are just like that of walking.

Straight running exercise. A good exercise is to find a gentle, easy slope, then send yourself straight down, weight evenly divided on both skis, arms at your sides for balance (left). Without changing position, flex the knees (opposite, top), then come up again (opposite, bottom). Repeat and repeat, up and down. This will help you become familiar with the necessity of keeping your knees soft.

You are looking for a rhythm and a tempo of your own. Some people have longer legs, others have shorter ones. If they try to copy each other, or go step for step they will not develop their own natural rhythm. Rather, they should try to build their own speed. In other words, do their own thing at their own pace and tempo.

The idea of the glide is to extend it further and further so you are able to move ahead at your own speed. Glide on the skis rather than walk on them. Your own motion at your own tempo. Relate back to ice skating again—push, glide; push, glide. One, two; one, two.

Do not let the heel "get ahead." In other words, don't try to reach your stride too far. If you let your heel get too far ahead, look what happens to your knee. The leg straightens out and you end up with what I call a lost ski. You cannot step down on a lost ski.

So limit your stride so that, at all times, the ball of the foot is down when you push off.

Another way to check this is to limit the length of your stride to the length of your legs to be sure the back leg's foot is down and you can put all of your weight on that ski to push off.

The camber of the ski is such that if you don't have all of the weight on that ski, you cannot utilize the wax job or the artificial base on that ski to keep it from sliding backwards. You have to have all of your weight, the entire body weight, on the ball of the foot in order to get the thrust that comes from the push-off.

Your balance will come automatically when you ski without poles. So skiing back and forth without poles is recommended for many skiers. Even some of the best skiers in the world will, at times early in the season, ski without poles to regain their natural balance.

After you are more accomplished on your skis, here is an exercise you will want to do. It is done from time-to-time by very fine skiers because it is an excellent conditioner. It is called "quick ski": While keeping your arms at about a 90-

Look ahead one ski length or more.

degree angle, ski with short, quick strides. Let the back of the ski come up high if it has a tendency to do so. You should have the feeling of developing a strong kick. Be sure to quickly recover your legs after that kick is completed. After you get the feeling of the quick leg recovery, try to get the feeling that the hip swings with the knee forward like a pendulum.

I wouldn't overdo it, but it won't hurt to ski without poles quite often. Particularly early in the season, take a little walk without poles, and you will find that it is a lot easier. Everything will come very easy, particularly for beginners. After a while, you will say, "Why, I don't miss the poles at all!"

That is beautiful! You are standing there and you have developed all of your natural balance. You don't need the crutches at all, do you? Concentrate on looking ahead, flex your knees, correct your body position. Soften the knee as you step on the ski.

All of this comes when you are not using your poles. Everything falls into place and you can use the poles for the push forward rather than fighting it.

# 6
# Technique

There are three basic steps to cross-country skiing: The diagonal, the uphill, and the downhill.

**The Diagonal**
In Chapter 5 I mentioned the diagonal and defined it as alternate stride. The most important part of it is the complete transfer of weight from left to right; from right to left. Practice shifting your body weight from ski to ski on each glide. This is an excellent exercise to help further develop your balance. Remember that all of the weight goes on the ball of one foot, so the diagonal becomes a two-legged motion—the push-off with the leg that had the weight on the ball of the foot, and the push forward with the pointed knee of the opposite leg. Step over, or transfer the weight to the forward ski and glide.

This double-leg is a very much neglected point, but it is one of the most important in cross-country skiing. Push forward—and I do mean push forward—with the pointed knee. This will enable you to glide more, or to glide at all. Without the

35

transfer of weight, you simply cannot push off. Without the transfer of weight, you cannot get the camber of your skis to reach down and grip the snow, which is necessary for the push. Without the transfer of weight, you may even go backwards.

Also you could not have a forward motion on that opposite leg unless you form a platform, which comes automatically from transfer of weight. You cannot force the knee pointed forward without having something from which to push off. It just won't work. This transfer of weight is so important I cannot stress it enough.

From the push-off, of course, there will be a glide. As you transfer your weight from ski to ski and push, you will find you will be trying more and more to extend the glide and, if you are doing it right, you will be gliding farther. A little later on, as you become more proficient, I will tell you how to get some valuable help from the poles.

In the meanwhile, here is an exercise that will help you utilize the push-off more. First, lay your poles down. Take a few small, little jogging steps, then suddenly a push with the right foot. Glide for a while on both skis. Now repeat with the opposite foot.

**SKIING WITHOUT POLES.** This is one of your first exercises and serves to familiarize you with the motion of the skis as well as the natural rhythm that will develop as you become more efficient in your skiing. This skiing without poles is an excellent way to learn balance and to avoid dependence on poles as crutches.

Push-off, then glide; push-off, glide, keeping in mind the two-legged motion. If you keep your arms loose and forget they are there, you will find more and more that they are helping you. They will, all by themselves, swing forward and help with the push-off. They will do this automatically in a natural, rhythmic motion. When you realize this, it will be a very pleasant surprise. Many times people have a problem with their hands. They will say their hands don't feel right, and they try to force them into a position.

So let your arms hang down very loosely. Soon you are going to find that, while concentrating on the motion of your legs, the arms are going to move normally, in a very natural motion. This is the rhythm you want and, once you have got the rhythm, you can always stretch the stride and extend the motion of your arms more. Remember, the arms should go back past your hips, then swing forward.

Now is the time to pick up the poles again. You will find yourself looking at them for the first time in a different way. Remember, at the beginning you tried to use them as a crutch to hold yourself up. But you don't need them that way anymore. You have developed a natural balance, which, of course, is much better, and it came because you skied without your poles.

When you pick the poles up they will probably seem very long at first, and they are, so let me explain why they are of this length. When doing the diagonal, if you set the poles

**PUSH AND GLIDE.** This exercise is designed to help you accomplish your first glide. It is a simple jogging motion, pushing off with one leg then gliding on both skis. This is the basis for all cross-country skiing. Learning the kick-off is an important feature of one phase of skiing.

down in front of your foot, they will fight your forward motion, but you can use them as an asset. Because of their length and by putting them down at the right and proper angle, you can push the correct way and help yourself move forward.

Of course, when you are cross-country skiing, you will have a thrust of the poles with every glide. You may ask how far

**STEPPING AROUND HEELS AND TOE.** Learn the balance of your skis by picking up the tip of the right ski, moving it a few inches to the left, putting it down and bringing the left ski parallel to it. Repeat until you have moved in a full circle (left). Do the same thing going to the left. Then repeat both again, this time lifting your heels first (right).

forward do you plant the pole? The basic rule that I tell my students at the Sun Valley Nordic Ski School is: The poles should be set out in such a way that the tip of the pole, that point below the wire ring at the bottom, should go no further forward than the opposite toe. In other words, when you take a step, your left toe and your right hand should be at the same forward place, just opposite each other. Then, of course, with your next step, your right toe and your left hand will be equal distant forward. Practice that for a minute or two; swing your arm forward to the extended forward position while, at the

same time, stepping forward with the opposite foot.

Do this again, only this time, bend the forward arm just slightly. Remember, your hand should be carried pretty low. Look at the angle the pole makes. This is the proper angle.

Get used to that angle by swinging your poles, moving them back and forth just the same way you moved your arms before picking up the poles. That's right, get a little rhythm going. Fine.

Stand still now, tighten the strap on the poles, then push the poles down. You don't have to hang on to them hard. Remember that your hand can be loose because the strap is there. Hold on to the poles in a way so that the rings are behind and down, keeping them at about a 45-degree angle. Move them back and forth, but off the snow, and get that rhythm. Swing your arms forward and back past your hip. Stand still while you are doing this little exercise, but keep your knees soft. Continue until you get to know how it feels to get the rhythm swinging your arms with the poles in your hands. You will find that by keeping your knees soft, your whole body will get into the swing of cross-country skiing.

Now just ski the snow. Instead of pushing with the poles, I would like to have you put your hand down low, have a little angle on the pole and allow the rings of the poles to drag. Right now you are only looking for one thing—rhythm.

Now you are skiing, dragging the poles, and beginning to feel a little of the rhythm.

You have probably noticed that I keep repeating the word rhythm. Rhythm is one of the most important parts of cross-country skiing. You will recall that I mentioned earlier that some people have long legs and others have short legs and the important thing is to develop your own tempo and speed and not to try to copy someone else. Copying won't work. Do your own thing in your own tempo. Try to develop something that is easy for you and feels good to you. If it is right for you, you can do it a long time. Even all day. So modify everything you learn to fit your own personal needs. Search for your own tempo, your own rhythm.

With that word rhythm firmly entrenched in your mind, we can go on and apply it to movement. You have poles in hand and are transferring your weight from ski to ski in rhythm with your knees soft. By now you should be a little more comfortable as you shift your weight from leg to leg, foot to foot, ski to ski. You are letting your hands move in a natural way with the poles. So you are ready to develop the use of the poles a little further.

Take a step, plant the pole down at a point about opposite the opposite foot; set it there instead of dragging it. Set it down and push. Eventually you want the pole to help with

**THE TOURING STRIDE.** The touring stride is a motion of left leg/right arm, right leg/left arm synchronization. Be sure to plant the front pole at an angle to take advantage of the push it offers. The stride should be developed into an easy-going rhythm. But the tempo should be suited to you, not to your partner.

that forward push. The combination of the pole-push and the kick-glide will carry you farther forward than just the glide. This is the natural alternate stride, called the diagonal. Each pole helps each time with each stride.

The motion will be left foot, right pole. Do this motion in front of a mirror. You are "striding on the diagonal." This is the same natural motion you did when you were skiing without poles. The poles are there now and will be of help when you push off.

The poles should be a part of you and synchronized with your leg motion. In a natural movement, your arm should be bent slightly, not straight. You want and need the strength from your arms, and a straight arm doesn't have any strength

**ADVANCED STRIDE.** As you improve, you will be getting into the diagonal, which is an advanced stage of the touring stride. You will learn to exaggerate the step-glide. The push forward is very important here. You should be concentrating on the progressively advancing glide and the pointed-forward knees.

at all. So bend the arm a little bit and allow it to follow through in a natural way. Many people make the mistake of stopping their hands at the hip. Allow your arm to go all the way past your hip, then open your hand, almost releasing your grip on the pole. Your hand should be quite open, so that you are holding on to the pole with only the tips of a couple fingers plus the strap.

Earlier you learned how to put the strap on. Now you can see why: It will help bring the pole back. Regrab the pole and you are ready for the next push.

Of course when I say regrab the poles, I don't really mean grab. You want a light but firm grip. If you see somebody with his or her pole pointed straight up in the air, you know right away he or she is hanging on for life. You also know that person cannot be utilizing the poles in the proper way and will become very tired in the arms and hands.

Another exercise that will help you to develop your diagonal is called a "two-step diagonal." To begin, do a series of regular diagonal strides: Take a step, plant the right pole down at a point about opposite the left foot, which is at the bottom of a soft, pointed knee. With the right ski, which is the back ski, push forward. Glide. Transfer your weight to the left ski. Repeat with the opposite arm and leg. You have that down pretty well now, so I want you to just add a glide. That's right, an unassisted, free ride, so to speak. Do one left, then one right diagonal stride, then do a left glide then a right glide without the aid of the poles. Repeat the entire cycle again. When you are practicing this, count to yourself—pole, pole, glide, glide, pole, pole, glide, glide.

This is a nice change of pace from the usual diagonal stride.

## Uphill

You can see how natural cross-country skiing is. Nothing to be afraid of, and so easy when you do it right. Easy? Yes! The diagonal, or alternate stride, you just learned is probably used for 90 percent of your skiing. That's right, even when going uphill.

Unless you live in an area where the land is flat as a Swedish pancake, you will have to do some skiing uphill. It is not as difficult as you might think; and, in fact, many people say it is easier to go uphill on cross-country skis than it is to climb up on foot. Maybe that's because we go the easiest way up and expend the least amount of energy. I like to use what I call the "direct approach." In other words, I like to say ski as far as you can with a glide.

When I'm going straight up, I like to ski with nothing but

Going straight uphill.

the regular diagonal stride: Push off, glide. Depending upon the steepness of the slope, I probably will have to shorten my stride a little bit and push a little harder, remembering the important pointed knee. I like to continue my gliding motion, even if I'm climbing, as long as possible.

When you are skiing uphill, be careful to not allow your body to go too far back. Your upper body should be a little more erect, with a very slight forward lean and the hips well forward. Also, when you are skiing uphill, the forward knee should be bent more than when you are skiing on the flat.

**STRAIGHT UP.** When the hill is not too steep, you can ski straight up with your normal touring stride. As the slope gets steeper, you may have to shorten your stride and, finally, lift your skis and set them down to continue your forward upward progress. The last motion will some-what resemble a jogging movement. Lean forward over your skis.

When you get to a hill that is too steep to get a good glide, you can still go on by picking up the skis and setting them down. It is a simple straight-up, straight-down, running-in-place motion, except you are moving forward, always forward! This method helps you get a little better grip on the snow. In this motion, the poles should be kept behind to protect you from slipping backwards and to help in the regular pushing motion.

Pick up the skis and set them straight down.

As you continue to climb, use the same rhythm, but with less of everything—a shortened stride and less glide. It will become progressively harder to do and you will have to push a little more until finally you won't have any glide at all and will be walking up. If you are doing it right, you will not slide backwards. That is why you have the wax, or a mohair, fish scale, or step pattern on the bottoms of your skis.

If the slope becomes steeper and you cannot go straight up anymore, you would use the side-stepping, straight-up technique. This is a very easy motion: Just turn sideways so the skis sit across, or perpendicular to, the slope. All you do now is pick up the skis and side-step, ski by ski, up the hill.

**SIDE-STEPPING UPWARD.** A simple way to go
up. Be sure to keep your skis across the slope. Keep
skis as evenly balanced as possible when lifting; don't
allow the tail to drift down. If necessary, turn your knees and
ankles slightly into the hill to keep from slipping down. Extend your
arms and poles out to the side for balance as you step sideways up the hill.

Transfer your weight to the downhill ski and lift the uphill
ski sideways and up. Set that ski down, transfer weight to it,
then lift the downhill ski and bring it alongside. Repeat until
you are up the hill.

Don't worry about slipping down, even though you really
don't have hard edges on your cross-country skis. If the snow
is soft, you can almost altogether forget the possibility of slipping because, if you remember, soft snow grips. If the snow is
hard, you will need all of the edges you have, so learn how to
use them. The way to do that is to simply turn the skis
slightly into the hill. Or, I can tell you to turn the knees and
ankles slightly into the hill and you will have "an edge."

By turning the knees and ankles toward the hill, you will

automatically be on the uphill edges—the gripping edges—of the skis. Then, using the edges, just walk up sideways.

Another way up the hill is to side-step forward. I call this "cutting down the mountain." So, to cut down the mountain, step forward and up, ringing the mountain and, thus, cutting down the steepness of the slope. Again, use the edges of your skis by turning the knees and ankles into the hill. The poles are always behind helping to push all the time.

**SIDE-STEP FORWARD**. This is the same motion as side-stepping upward, except you are moving forward as well as up. This is one of many ways to cut down a hill. Don't let the poles interfere with your step by holding them too close to your body.

A hill also may be climbed on cross-country skis using the herringbone. I am sure you have heard of this technique because the name is very appropriate. If you stand away from the hill and look at the imprint left by the skis, you will see a pattern that looks like a herring's backbone.

The way to do a herringbone is to put the skis into a V position with the tips apart; a position I call either a "back-

Leif leads a group herringboning up a hill.

wards snowplow" or an "opposite wedge." Put your poles be-hind and just walk up in that position. Lift the ski forward while leaning a little forward, just enough so that it won't cross the other ski in the back. Step on the ski, bend the knee, then lift the opposite ski in the same manner. That is how to herringbone up a hill.

**HERRINGBONE.** Herringbone is an easy way to conquer a big hill. Be sure to keep body weight forward and use the inside edges of your skis with the poles behind as you step forward and up. You will leave a track that resembles a fish's skeleton.

If you have heard or read anything about sailboating, you are probably familiar with the term "tacking." For hikers it is know as "switchbacking." The basic movement is to travel in a back and forth manner, something like a continuous series of Zs. This is an excellent way to cut down a hill that is too steep to go straight up or even to herringbone. So you are

**TACKING.** Tacking is another method of cutting down the size of a mountain you are trying to climb. If you were hiking, you would call this a switchback, because it is nothing more than zigzagging up a hill.

going to go in traverse, across the hill, in one direction, then change the pattern by turning around. To get to the opposite direction traverse, get into a herringbone position—the opposite wedge—so you won't slide back. Also, set your poles behind you as an extra precaution from sliding back. Then just step turn around and start back across the hill in a slightly uphill, zigzag pattern.

You may be wondering why we have to learn so many methods of getting up a hill. The reason is that we have to be our own ski lift.

In going uphill remember to take your time. Rest; look at the beauty of the scenery. Enjoy everything surrounding you and do not rush up to the top. This is an important part of touring or cross-country skiing. Enjoy nature wherever you ski.

### Downhill

All well and good thus far. You have come a long way and are happily on top of a hill. Fine. You have, of course, heard that old expression, "What goes up must come down." You are no different, and it is time for you to go down the hill. The first thing to consider is where to go down; selection of terrain is very important. Look around and find a suitable place, one that is not too steep. You want a small, gentle slope that has a minimum of trees and other potential hazards.

Once you find the right place, the easiest way to go to the bottom is straight down. That's right, just straight down. If you are an Alpine skier, this won't startle you because you already know how to do that. So these instructions will be sort of a refresher course for you.

The downhill position is very basic: Set the skis in a comfortable, normal shoulder-wide position, approximately six to seven inches apart. Your upper body should have a slight forward lean from the hip, arms hanging loose. Your weight should be evenly divided on both skis. Bend your knees and ankles slightly forward; keep them soft, flexible. But remember one thing, particularly if you happen to be an Alpine skier:

Straight running downhill.

You have been told many times to force the knees forward. Do *not* do that here. That force causes the heel to come up and, if you are on cross-country skis, you will end up on your toes. When that happens, you will lose your balance right away. So keep your heels down, weight on the ball of the foot and evenly divided on both skis.

All set? Lift the poles out of the snow and keep your arms and poles away from the body. Soften the knees with a little up and down motion. Just bounce slightly. Look ahead, see where you are going to go. Remember, looking ahead and not down at your skis helps you keep your balance better, in addition, of course, to seeing what lies in your path. All right now, give a little push and just glide down.

See how easy it is?

Straight running exercise. Leif Odmark demonstrates the straight running position (below, left), then adds an exercise (below, right) on a gentle slope. He is practically gliding, then (opposite page) picks up one ski, either the entire ski or just the back, and holds. Do the same with the opposite ski. This is very good for your balance.

That is what we call the straight, running way down. There is another way to go straight down the hill using a "snowplow." The snowplow motion is a break with which you can slow down, check your speed and, eventually, come to a stop.

The first thing to do is to take the snowplow position standing still: Put the skis in a wedge; the heels are apart, the tips are fairly close, about four to five inches apart in front. Bend your knees forward, the same as in the downhill position. Keep your weight evenly divided on both skis and on the balls of the feet. Your arms should hang loosely, your whole position relaxed, and your skis flat on the snow. Pick up the poles.

I like to maintain my skis in this snowplow position all the way down the hill because it gives me good control over my speed. But be careful to keep your weight evenly distributed on both skis. If you step more on one ski than the other, you are going to lose control.

Snowplow position. A snowplow is a wedge with the tips together. Practice this position on the flat so it won't feel strange when you take this stand on a hill. Flex your knees and ankles, and keep your weight even on both skis.

The snowplow is appropriately named. Some people also call it a wedge, which is an accurate name, too, but I prefer the term snowplow. What this snowplow does is basically what any snowplow does, and that is to push the snow out of the way. When you do that while skiing, your snowplow breaks the speed at which you are traveling, actually slowing you down.

Let's go over the snowplow again: Your knees should be bent forward, your weight evenly divided on both skis, tips four to five inches apart. Keep your heels down and your body with a slight forward lean. Pick up your poles, keeping your arms away from your body. Look ahead. If the snow is soft, you can ski on a very flat ski. As you go, there should be a slight scraping motion on the inside edge of the ski. You accomplish this by turning your knees and ankles in slightly. Be

**SNOWPLOW EXERCISE.**
Start at the top of a gentle
slope in the straight, running
position. Bend knees and
ankles forward, keeping your
weight evenly divided on
both skis. Push the heels
and the backs of the skis out
into the snowplow position.
Once you are in the position,
come up slightly in the
knees—not all the way—and
the skis will automatically
come back parallel again.
Repeat. This exercise is very
important before you start
learning to turn.

careful not to overturn the knees. If you turn your knees in too much, the skis are going to run in together and you are going to be sitting in the snow wondering what happened. You were riding on the edges, that's what happened. So that means you are going to have to flatten the skis a little more to scrape them and to keep them in the snowplow position all the way down the hill.

If you edge one ski or the other or both too much by turning your knees and ankles in too much, your skis are going to cross in front. And that spells disaster. It is a matter of learning to control the edges. This is worthwhile to spend some time on, because you can combine the snowplow with other motions.

For example, if the slope is steep, you may start out in the straight running position and ski that way until you think you are going too fast. Then, control your speed by going into a snowplow position. When you have the speed under control and feel comfortable again, come up in the knees a little bit, which causes the skis to run parallel again automatically. You can continue in the straight running position or alternate between that and the snowplow all the way down, and be perfectly safe with your speed under control.

Traversing is another good way to get down the slope. It is something like a switchback or tacking motion that we often employ as an uphill technique. In a traverse, you actually cut down the steepness of the hill by cutting the angle of the slope. Let me describe it this way: Instead of going straight down, you go sideways at an angle across the slope which, by the very nature of it, makes you go less fast.

In traversing, you should be in the straight running position: Skis set in the normal shoulder-wide position, approximately six to seven inches apart, and your weight evenly divided on both skis. Your knees should be bent slightly forward and kept soft and flexible. The main difference between the downhill and the traverse positions is that, instead of keeping your skis even, as in straight down, always keep one ski, the uphill ski or the ski that is closest to the hill, slightly ahead.

**TRAVERSE.** Traversing a mountain means to ski across the face at an angle, thus cutting the degree of steepness. Try for a nice diagonal rather than pointing your skis too much down the slope. Your position should be: weight evenly divided on both skis, the uphill ski slightly ahead, knees bent, ankles flexible—and keep your poles away from your body but do not allow them to drag in the snow. Look ahead. If your skis are slipping sideways down the hill, turn your knees and ankles slightly into the hill. This simple action will allow you to "hold an edge" and continue your traverse.

If you have soft snow, keep your weight evenly divided on both skis. If the snow is hard, you should have a little more weight on the downhill ski. But don't worry too much about traversing because, in cross-country skiing, you don't have the support of either the high, locked-in-place boots or the sharp edges of Alpine skis.

What do you do, you may ask, if the hill is too steep for any of these methods? I would say to look around and find a slope with a less severe angle. If you find a hill that you think ought to be right for you and you ski it several times and fall each time, that is a pretty good indication right there that the slope is, indeed, too steep for you. In that case, I would go and look for another that is gentle and ski that enough to regain confidence.

What if you don't have a choice and have to go down a slope you know is too steep for you to handle? You can always side-step down. The motion is exactly the same as when you side-stepped up; you are just doing it in the opposite direction, going down instead of up. With your knees and ankles pointed into the hill to give you an edge, pick up your downhill ski and move it sideways several inches; put it down. Bring the other ski down next to it. Literally inch your way down the slope.

Also, depending upon snow conditions and steepness of the slope, you probably will need to use the edges of your skis. Remember to just point your knees and ankles into the hill to get an edge.

If the slope is very steep and you are at a point where you feel very uncomfortable, you can always take your skis off and walk down.

And, while we are still talking about going downhill, if you are a beginner, *never* put the poles in front of the body trying to stop. You could hurt yourself pretty badly by jamming the poles in front of you because a pole could hit or slam into your stomach.

If you feel you are going too fast and you cannot handle the speed, simply sit down. Just relax and sit. Let the body slow the speed. All of the cross-country ski equipment is soft and you will not hurt yourself. Don't panic, don't fling yourself, don't try to catch yourself with the poles. Just sit down.

Equipment is soft, so falling does not hurt.

## Turns

Once you have mastered the diagonal, uphill, and downhill to a moderate degree of proficiency, you will begin enjoying the sport of cross-country skiing and touring. To further enhance your pleasure in challenging the winter wonderland, you should learn to command basic turns.

In order to understand the use of various turns, the skier must understand what the "fall line" is. This is an imaginary line that goes straight downhill from top to bottom on any hill or slope of any size. To determine the fall line, think of dropping a golf ball or a snowball from the top. The ball will roll straight down along what we call the fall line, the line along which something falls down the hill.

When we discussed downhill, we were not concerned with turning. Now it is time to learn that phase of cross-country skiing. The first change of direction you will learn is called the "stepturn." This a very safe turn used by some of the best skiers at any time. Standing still, you can get the feel of this turn by picking up the left ski and moving the tip of the ski to the left three or four inches, setting it down, and bringing the other ski to it. Regain your balance by standing on both skis before you make the next motion. Now repeat.

Feel familiar? It should because, if you will recall when you first put on your skis, we did this in an exercise. We picked up the tips and moved them around in a circle. This is the very

**STEP TURN.** Since this is your first turn, pick a very gentle slope and move very slowly. Gradually change directions by lifting your left ski up and over a few inches; bring right ski parallel. Repeat, regaining your balance as necessary.

same thing—a step turn. Gradually, as you are moving and want to turn to the left, you would pick up your left ski, move it to the left, perhaps five to six inches. Bring your right ski parallel to it. Continue and you will gradually change directions to the left.

Once you have picked up the left ski, you are probably going to feel that you will lose your balance. Most beginners rush this motion. Bring the right ski to the left, then stand for a while to regain your balance, feel comfortable before taking the next step.

This same step turn can, of course, be repeated to the right. Pick up your right ski first and move it five to six inches to the right, bring your left ski up parallel, regain your balance and repeat.

For a step turn, the poles are usually picked up out of the snow. You really don't need the poles, so you will probably want to have them away from your body for balance. Be comfortable with them. Do not drag them. Rather lift them up, away from the snow.

The "kick turn" is another method of changing direction

that is done standing. It is not as easy as the step turn and, in fact, can be a little tricky at first, so take your time. Don't rush because once you have practiced it, you will wonder why it seemed so complicated. This is one movement you might want to try without skis first, just to get the feel of it.

To do a kick turn, begin with your skis parallel, weight shifted to the right ski. Turn your body so it faces to the left. Put both poles behind you on either side of your body. Pick up your left ski, swing it around a complete 180 degrees so it is facing the opposite direction (backwards from your right ski), and set it down. There you are, standing with both poles behind you, your left ski facing left and your right ski facing right. Stay that way for a moment to regain your balance. Now, with your weight on the left ski and using your left pole for balance, swing your right ski around so it is parallel to the left and set it down. You are now facing in the opposite direction from where you started.

Try it again, this time to the right. With your weight on your left ski, pick up your right one and swing it around so it faces in the opposite direction. Now pick up the left and set it down parallel to the right again. See, it really is that easy.

Now you will learn to make a turn while you are in motion. There are many different motion turns, so let's begin with a simple one that I like to call "ski around the corner."

**SKIING AROUND THE CORNER.** When changing direction while in the touring or diagonal stride, you simply ski around the corner. It helps to remember that you can sneak around the corner, too, and that you can bend down a little lower. Remember to keep gliding all of the time.

Move along in your regular touring stride, at a nice and easy pace. Pick out a spot where you want to make a turn. Now, instead of stopping there and making a step turn, pick up a ski and turn it toward the direction you want to go, all the while continuing to move in your touring stride.

Skiing around the corner, then, is just exactly the same movements you do when you walk around a corner. Pick up one ski, your right one, for example, and set it down in the direction you want to turn. Follow that by picking up your left and setting it back down parallel to the right, all the while continuing your touring stride. In a word, bend your knees and sort of sneak around the corner while continuing your forward motion.

The motion for the next turn is very similar to that of ice skating, so it is called the "skate turn." The skate turn uses the inside edge of the ski to push off, then you glide and bring your skis together again.

To do a skate turn, start with one double pole movement. Reach out with both poles, set them down, and push with them. Glide on both skis, with your weight evenly distributed between both. Bend slightly into a crouch and push off in the

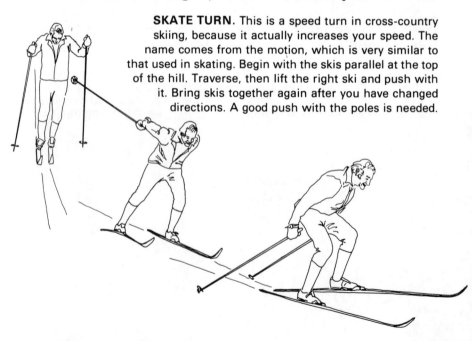

**SKATE TURN.** This is a speed turn in cross-country skiing, because it actually increases your speed. The name comes from the motion, which is very similar to that used in skating. Begin with the skis parallel at the top of the hill. Traverse, then lift the right ski and push with it. Bring skis together again after you have changed directions. A good push with the poles is needed.

direction you want to go. Pick up one ski, either the left or the right, while the opposite leg pushes off. Then transfer the body weight over to the other ski. Swing both arms forward for the next double pole forward movement. Bring the other ski parallel and the turn is completed. You again have your weight on both skis and the direction has been changed.

Let's go over that again. Stand on both skis, weight evenly divided, and prepare for a double pole motion. Push off. Change the direction of the left ski. Go into a crouch position. With the right ski, using the inside edge, push yourself forward, push off. Bring the right ski up to the left and stand on both skis again. Thus the movement is completed.

If you are turning to the left, just repeat the movement using the opposite leg.

Remember when you were learning to go downhill you used a method called a snowplow? Now you are going to expand your knowledge of the snowplow and learn to use it in making turns. This, of course is called the "snowplow turn." You will recall that a snowplow depends on the use of the heels. You are in the wedge-type snowplow position with the weight evenly divided on both skis, and you push out with your heels.

Now, before trying the snowplow turn, I would like to have you do a little exercise to become better acquainted with the idea that the heels are actually pushed out. I mentioned earlier that when the skis are in a straight snowplow, your knees and ankles are bent forward, and your heels are down. If you come up a little in the knees, you will find the skis automatically run parallel again. It does not require any other movement from you except coming up a little in the knees and you come out of the wedge just like that. That probably taught you something. If you push the knee a little more forward, making an attempt to push the heels apart, you can do just that. The heels do push rather easily.

So in this exercise you will start out in a parallel position and let the skis run down a little hill. Now, press your knees forward, push your heels down and push out into the snowplow position. Come up in the knees and the skis will be running parallel again. Do this several times as an exercise to get the feeling that you can push the heels out anytime you please.

After doing this exercise several times, you can get into the regular snowplow turn. Start out in the snowplowing position, weight evenly divided between both skis. Transfer your weight slightly to the right ski and watch what happens.

Let me say it another way: Push the heel out a little more on the right ski to start, then stay quite square over both skis, staying in the middle. Push out the right heel a little more and transfer a little more weight to the right ski. See what is happening? That's right! You find yourself turning to the left.

Don't worry about the left ski, it will follow right along. It is important to keep both skis in the plowing position all of the time. Don't push one ahead. A lot of beginners make the mistake of trying to push one ski in front of the other, trying to force it. The only thing that does is to make the skis cross all the time, and you know what happens then. So keep both ski tips fairly close together all the time you are in the snowplow position.

If you are in the right position but find that your skis do not turn, it probably is because of the edges. You are probably edging too much. In other words, you cannot scrape the skis along at all; you cannot move the heels at all. So you know right then and there that the knees are turned in too much and that you are riding on the edges. The edges of your skis were sticking in the snow and that's why you couldn't move them. They were probably running together and crossing, too. The skis were edged too much and the knees were too stiff. So bend your knees and ankles and flatten the skis a little more so you will be able to slide them. That's part of the snowplow position.

Let's go over the snowplow turn again: Put your skis in a wedge, weight evenly divided, keeping your body fairly in the middle. Lean a little forward over the skis and stay in the middle. Start transferring your weight to one ski, then slowly

**SNOWPLOW TURN.** Assume the basic snowplow position and begin a traverse across a slope. Begin with weight evenly divided on both skis, then, as you start your turn, shift your weight to the downhill, or turning, ski as you bend your knees and ankles forward. Lean sideways slightly over the downhill ski. Maintain the snowplow, or wedge, position at all times. Make small, little turns in the fall line at first, then later develop a larger, sweeping turn.

put more weight on the ski while continuing the pushing-with-the-heel motion. That's like going downhill. Depending upon the steepness of the slope, you will put more and more weight on the downhill ski. If the slope is very steep, you will want to be leaning over that turning ski.

But be sure to keep your knees soft. If you take your weight off the turning ski or straighten up your knees, you are going to lose the turning ski; it is going to go straight down. Then you are in trouble.

When you start out making turns, you should begin with a very narrow snowplow, with the heels not very far apart. This makes the edges a little flatter.

Also at first, do not make too many turns. Make a small turn before trying to make a severe turn. Just change the direction a little bit. Then lean more, shift your weight. Be easy at first and do not expect too much. Practice just one or two small little changes of direction as you go down the hill.

The next turn is called the "stem turn" and is based on the snowplow. Have the snowplow turn well in mind and be able to execute it without difficulty before you tackle this one.

Begin your stem turn on a moderately gentle slope. Start out in your traverse position, going across the hill left, with your skis parallel, weight evenly divided. To start the turn, which would be to the right, put your weight on your right ski and pick up the left, or uphill, ski and plant it in the direction of your turn. This will put the skis in the position of a half snowplow. Then, gradually transfer your body weight to the left ski, which now becomes the turning ski. Be sure your left knee is soft and bent. The body should lean over the left ski very slightly, as the ski turns from the fall line into the new direction. As the turn is completed, the right ski is brought in parallel to the left ski and you are back in the traverse position, weight evenly divided, going in the opposite direction.

Of course, to make a turn to the left, everything will be exactly the opposite. You start across the hill traversing to the right, with skis parallel, weight evenly divided. Shift your

**STEM TURN.** The stem turn is more advanced than the snowplow and employs a half snowplow. Traverse, weight on the downhill ski. Pick up the uphill ski and plant it so the tip is in and the heel out. Shift your weight to the ski you have just planted and you will be into your turn. As you complete the turn, let the skis run in parallel traverse position again.

weight to your left ski, pick up the right, or uphill, ski, and plant it in the direction you want to turn. Remember, your position here should look like a half snowplow. Gradually shift your body weight to the right ski, keeping that knee soft. Lean the body slightly over the right ski. After turning, bring the left ski back parallel to the right and divide your weight evenly again.

After some practice, you will not need to open your uphill ski nearly as much. We call that stemming smaller, which enables you to make stem turns with more speed.

The "telemark" turn was the first turn skiers ever made. It originated in the Scandinavian countries, then was borrowed, along with the other basic skiing maneuvers, by Alpine countries. That is why downhill skiing is referred to as "Alpine."

Telemark is a pretty fancy word for a basic position. If you recall, you did some warm-up exercises that involved getting down on one knee. Well, that is just about the basic telemark position. Stand on both skis, weight evenly divided between them. Slide the left ski ahead with the right one back. The left knee should be right over the front ski, while the right ski tip is approximately at the instep of the left foot, right heel well off the ski. Hold it right there; that is the telemark position.

Telemark position.

This position will vary in length, depending upon how it is being used. You will use it in a number of different terrains, skiing over dips and holes, for example.

The first thing you should do is practice your telemark position in straight running before you ever attempt to turn. You can do this by picking a very gentle slope and going straight down, alternating telemark positions from left to right. Push your left ski forward, straighten up again, then push your right ski forward. Of course, your knees have to be very soft to do this exercise. Before trying any turns, learn this basic position first and practice it several times. Help yourself to balance by using your poles. Set them in the snow at the side each time you go down.

**TELEMARK TURN.** Now, after you have done the telemark exercise, do the same basic movement to make the turn. Keep your weight evenly divided on both skis, skis slightly edged in the direction of the turn. Be sure to keep knees soft, and the rear ski tip tucked in the instep of the forward boot. Push left ski forward for the right turn, as you assume the basic telemark position. The right ski will follow as you change directions.

When you feel fairly confident that you are doing the straight telemark position correctly, you can go into telemark turns. You will find that it is much easier to turn the first time from a slight traverse position rather than directly in the fall line. Start by turning the ski tips in the direction you want to make your turn. That little bit of steering is the beginning of the turn. Of course, the knees have to be very soft and flexible at all times. With the knee bent and the forward foot directly beneath the knee, keep your weight evenly divided on both skis, although you will find this will vary from time-to-time. Remember, the rear ski tip should be tucked in the instep of the forward boot to prevent the skis from crossing during the turn. There, that wasn't too difficult now, was it? Practice this again and again.

Now that you have successfully turned from a traverse, try this same telemark turn from the fall line. Start moving straight down the fall line. Pick up the poles and keep your arms out to the sides to help maintain your balance. Assume the telemark position. Point the tip of the left ski slightly in the direction you want to turn, in this case it will be to the right. As I mentioned earlier, the weight should be kept evenly divided on both skis if possible. You are going to be in for a very pleasant surprise—you are turning just like that.

Remember, do not rush these turns. Take your time. Make long, sweeping turns. A telemark turn requires fine balance and lots of practice. When you feel confident on the gentle slope where you started, move on to a steeper hill. This is just the beginning of a lot of fun for you.

If you want to have some fun while developing your competence in turning, set up a slalom course on an easy and gentle slope. The slalom is, of course, primarily used in Alpine racing, but it is an excellent training for cross-country skiers. Select a natural course, track, or path down a slope, or set up a course of gates. Mark certain places along the route—maybe some tall weeds sticking up through the snow, a bump, or almost anything that can be seen. Weave your way down the course, turning left around the first obstacle, then right around the second, then left again, and so forth until you get to the bottom. Put the gates, or obstacles, pretty wide to begin with. As I said, this is good practice as well as being a lot of fun.

Telemark slaloms are becoming more accepted in cross-country racing. So why not start your training right here and now? Who knows, you may be a telemark slalom cross-country ski champion just waiting to be discovered.

## Poles

You have been moving across the flat, going uphill, downhill, and learning to make turns. Now it is time to supplement your movements with correct use of the poles. Poles are a great aid as well as being necessary to cross-country skiing.

Of course, you cannot expect to become an expert at cross-country skiing overnight, even with the aid of this book. It takes miles and miles of practice to perfect the stride and the glide. Nevertheless, by this time, you are probably feeling fairly comfortable and have had time to develop your own rhythm of cross-country skiing—working the stride with the pole. Originally you were skiing without poles, swinging your arms back and forth, looking for a rhythm. Now you have developed your own tempo, your own rhythm, based solely on the length of your legs.

As you already know, cross-country ski poles are a lot longer than Alpine ski poles. The reason for that is they are used in different ways. The Alpine poles are set in front and you ski around them. That explains why you see Alpine skiers coming out for the first time on cross-country skis putting their poles in front of them. Using cross-country poles in that manner makes them into a crutch instead of an aid. And furthermore, the poles planted in that direction will inhibit your forward motion.

Although we discussed poles as an integral part of the diagonal, I want to explain them as a separate entity.

Hold the poles lightly and hold them so the hand is forward, the ring behind, farther back than the ski. Pick up the

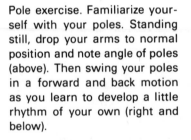

Pole exercise. Familiarize yourself with your poles. Standing
still, drop your arms to normal
position and note angle of poles
(above). Then swing your poles
in a forward and back motion
as you learn to develop a little
rhythm of your own (right and
below).

poles lightly in your hands, keeping them parallel, then move them back and forth as an extension of your arm as you develop a little rhythm. This is exactly the same thing you were doing when you swung your arms back and forth skiing without poles. Swing forward to almost level with your shoulder, swing back past your hip. Forward, back; forward, back.

Do not hang on to the poles. Keep a light grip.

At first, instead of pushing with the poles, drag them and think of only one thing—rhythm. Remember, you have to work the stride and the motion of your arms together, even if the poles are not involved.

Move a little across the snow; step, glide, step, glide. Swing your arms, forgetting the poles are there, just as you did when you skied without poles. Do not push at all. Just get the feeling. More than anything else, you want to develop your rhythm.

After you have made several passes gliding, the next thing you should do is begin to set the ring of the pole down and utilize a little push you get from that action. When you set the pole, you should not extend your hand so far forward that your arm becomes straight. Remember that you have no power with a straight arm. So keep your arm a little crooked, elbow pointed out a little bit so you have more strength. Bending your arm will also keep your poles a little closer to the body, as they should be. If you are skiing with the pole away from your body, you don't have any power again. So bring the hand a little closer so you feel more comfortable and have more power, which you can utilize in your push.

Another thing about your poles, you have probably noticed that the tips below the rings are slightly bent. This is not a defect in the pole, it was purposely made that way. Having the pole bent as it is, combined with the angle at which you set the pole in the snow and subsequently bring it back out of the snow, cuts the resistance and prevents the pole from getting stuck in the snow. This is particularly true when there is a crust of ice. Having the pole tip bent in such a way makes it release easier from the snow when you go to take it back for a new stride.

I mentioned earlier that you should not be grabbing on to the pole. You should have a soft grip. Let me explain why: The hand holding the pole is forward. When it goes back past your hip, it should open up, releasing the pole. So do not grab on to the pole; hold it easy so the hand can be just about completely open when it is back at the end of that stride. Let the strap bring the pole back so you can take hold again to set the pole down and give a little push at the beginning of your next stride. Develop your own rhythm; your own tempo. Tie the poles into that rhythm, synchronize them with your stride.

At this point, after trying this rhythm, you are likely to ask where to set the poles. That, of course, is a good question, one that indicates you are becoming more accustomed to having them in your hands. The answer I give students at the Sun Valley Nordic Ski School is that the rings of the poles should be set down no further forward than the toe of your opposite foot. In other words, as you stride out, your left toe and your right pole should be about even when they are forward on the diagonal. Your hand, of course, will be further ahead than the pole, so there will be an angle formed. Be careful, though, not to put the pole too far forward. If that happens, the pole will fight your forward motion.

There is another way to take advantage of your poles; it is called "double poling." To do double poling, stand on both skis and put both poles forward in the normal poling position—rings where the toes would be, hands ahead of that, forming the angle. Remember, if you put the rings too far forward, you will not be able to push and they will fight your forward motion. So put the poles down in such an angle that you actually can push, then follow through that push with your upper body bent forward and your arms moving back past your hips in a natural way. Remember to let your hands release the poles as they follow through. Also, keep your knees soft and your weight evenly divided on both skis while you are standing on the ball of the foot.

Now, do it again. Bring both arms forward and plant the poles opposite the toes. Push. Bend your upper body forward

**DOUBLE POLING.** Weight evenly divided on both skis, reach forward and grab with both poles. Push off with a good follow-through. Be sure to release both hands as they go back past your hips. This is a very nice motion on a slight downhill or any time you feel like it.

and allow your arms to follow through past your body. Release your grip on the poles.

There is no kick and glide with this, all of the motion comes from the double poling.

Double poling is used many times when you have a slight grade downhill and you find you are not going fast enough. Then you can help yourself by pushing with the double poling; pushing with both poles to gain a little speed. Also, you can double pole as a change of pace. If you have been doing the diagonal for a long time, then just throw in a couple double poling motions to change the whole pattern.

There is another poling action, "double poling with a kick," but you already know the elements of this because it is a combination of two basic motions. This can be taught a number of different ways. It can be taught standing still, for instance. Think of the exercise you did when we talked about pushing as a two-legged motion. The same thing comes into play here. Push off with the right leg and the pushing motion from the pointed left knee, poles down in the double poling position. Stand on both skis and ride for a while, then do the same thing again. Push off with the right leg and push forward with the left knee forward, both poles down in the double poling position, and follow through. Glide.

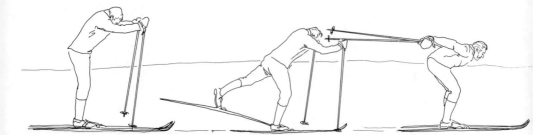

**DOUBLE POLING WITH A KICK.** This is the same basic movement as the double poling; only a kick has been added. Plant both poles in front, then, with a two-legged motion, push off with one ski as you head the other forward. Be sure to have the strap on your pole adjusted correctly. A good follow-through is important.

With a push-off that reminds you of ice skating, stand on both skis and glide. But in this case, you have two poles helping you along.

You can use double poling with a kick anytime you are on the flat and want to change the pace. You can also do it anytime you have a small downhill and want to get a good push to start. Or you can do it anytime you feel like it. A good time to do it is when there is a little hollow coming up, then an uphill. In this instance, I would do the double poling with a kick just before I got to the hollow to give myself a little more push to get a good start on the slope going uphill.

Practice double poling with a kick several times. Kick, then push with both poles. Practice this at first by using the same kicking leg, then practice alternating the kicking leg.

There is yet another double poling action, "double poling with two or more kicks." By this time, you already know I don't use fancy names for any of the exercises or techniques, therefore you know exactly what this motion is from its title. That's right, it is two or more kicks, then a push with both poles. Depending upon the terrain, you can get up a pretty good head of steam with this one. When skiing it, count to yourself: Kick, kick, poles; kick, kick, poles.

Now you know four methods of using your poles: the regular diagonal stride, the double poling, double poling with a kick, and double poling with two or more kicks.

But we aren't finished with the poles yet because I want to emphasize a few things. Do not hang on to the poles too hard. If you grab on to them, you will be like the many, many people, especially beginners, who complain after they are starting out that their hands, arms, and shoulders are tired. When I hear that complaint, I know that these people have used their poles as a crutch and have been hanging on to their poles for life without following through.

So it is important to adjust your straps so you can feel comfortable when you release the handles and know the straps will remain in place until you are ready to take up the poles again. Remember that in the follow-through, when your hand goes past your hip, release your hold on the pole; a couple fingers, at least, so there is little or nothing at all hanging on the pole at the moment your arm goes straight back. Then, let the strap bring the pole back. If you notice your pole pointing up in back, you know that you are hanging on too hard. So loosen up.

Everything in cross-country skiing should be loose. Very soft and loose. Very relaxed. I know this is easier said than done, but try to relax. If you stay relaxed, then you are going to get into your rhythm much easier and that rhythm is going to come easier if you relax more. Of course, it takes mileage for that rhythm to really develop, but the more skiing you can do, the more relaxed and comfortable you are going to get.

Now that you have your own rhythm, the poles are working correctly, and the stride is there, I am going to startle you. Forget the whole thing for a while and just ski. Ski for a couple of miles and just look around. If you will do that, you are going to find that everything about cross-country skiing is going to fall into place by itself.

Cross-country skiing is a very natural motion. Many people think of the one-two-three step and concentrate so hard on doing it right that they tense up. Forget all about that. Try to make skiing easy and simple. Make it easy on yourself; let

nature take over. You will find that the rhythm will work itself in all by itself. You have already practiced the basics properly, so let yourself go. After all, as I have said, cross-country
skiing is very, very natural.

# 7

# Equipment

You will recall that I suggested you rent skis at first. I think this is the only way to start for two important reasons: (1) You may not be sure at the beginning whether you actually like cross-country skiing well enough to spend money on equipment; and (2) until you have skied at least a time or two, you may not be sure exactly what you want—wax or nonwax skis, for instance.

If you have decided cross-country skiing is for you and owning your own equipment is the only way to ski, well then, read on.

In order to enjoy yourself and to have a good and carefree time, you must be outfitted correctly. That, of course, applies to renting as well as it does to owning. So when choosing your equipment, first of all consider the specific type of skiing you intend to do. The person who goes into cross-country racing will select and use different equipment than the person who only tours or the person who is a ski mountaineer.

The racer wants light and responsive equipment, he wants to carry the minimum weight and he has little concern for weather conditions because he is never away from other people for any length of time. At the opposite end of the scale is the ski mountaineer who carries a pack that may weigh as much as 60 pounds. He is exposed to all kinds of weather and has to rely on the equipment he can carry or put in his pack. He often is found at altitudes of more than 14,000 feet. He cares little about speed.

The ski tourer fits right in the middle of these two extremes. He seldom climbs mountains and, while he is both capable of and willing to carry packs that weigh as much as 45 to 50 pounds, he seldom packs more than 30 pounds on his back. I like to describe the ski tourer as the winter equivalent of the hiker, who has the ability to stay overnight if he wants to, but travels relatively light. Nevertheless, he is well prepared.

## Boots

I think the best place to start a discussion about equipment is with the boot. Boots are probably the most important piece of cross-country ski equipment you will buy. Why? First of all, the boot you pick will determine the type of equipment you will buy; and second, without good boots and a proper fit, you will not be able to fully enjoy the sport of cross-country skiing.

As I mentioned, the boot determines the rest of the equipment, so select your boots based on the type of skiing you want to do. It is true that just about any hiking or climbing boot is adaptable to touring, *if* you have the right binding to go with it.

There are boots made for almost every kind of condition of cross-country skiing. Some boots are insulated and are more comfortable in cold weather, but an extra pair of socks may solve the problem for the noninsulated boots.

Whatever you select, be sure you get a good fit. The boot should be snug in the heel and there should be plenty of room in the toes. Insist on good side-to-side rigidity. And there should be good flexibility over the ball of the foot.

Sometimes a beginner finds it difficult to make turns, particularly if the heel keeps slipping off the ski while he is mov-

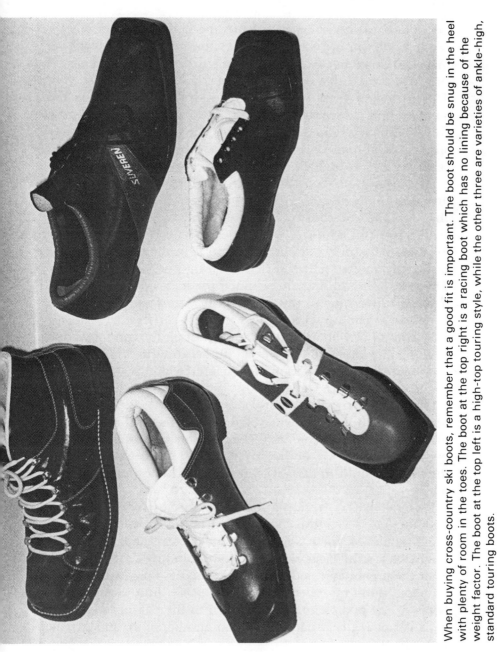

When buying cross-country ski boots, remember that a good fit is important. The boot should be snug in the heel with plenty of room in the toes. The boot at the top right is a racing boot which has no lining because of the weight factor. The boot at the top left is a high-top touring style, while the other three are varieties of ankle-high, standard touring boots.

ing. The fault may very well be in the boot. To check whether the boot you are looking at has the proper rigidity, take it in both hands and twist in opposite directions, as you would ring out a rag. The boot should be rigid and not twist. If it does turn and twist easily, the boot is poorly made, is too flexible, and whenever you attempt to make a turn skiing, your heel is likely to end up on the side of the ski rather than on it. A well-made boot has a metal piece along the bottom, between the sole and the foot to help maintain the rigidity.

Stay away from boots with either rubber or plastic uppers; they don't breathe and, as the result, your foot will get sweaty and wet and, of course, cold, too. The boot should have a leather top and a lining. When you try your boot on, simulate the diagonal stride and check the break in the boot (the crease across the toe) standing still. Lift your heel off the ground. The crease should not rub or touch the toes, nor should it feel tight. If it does any of these, do not buy that pair because you are likely to end up with blisters and very sore feet.

Be sure to buy boots that are long enough for comfort, but a little on the snug side in the width because they will expand and conform to your foot. If you are in doubt, pick a pair slightly too tight in width.

One characteristic all boots have in common is that they all open at the top and, when snow gets inside the boot and melts, the result is cold feet. This problem, however, can be overcome very easily by buying a pair of gaiters, which cover the top and hold tight against the legs, thus keeping the snow out.

I would like to caution all skiers about buying ski packages that include "everything you will need for cross-country skiing." Some of these sound like terrific bargains, and they might be for the basic skis, poles, and bindings. The problem with these packages is that you are usually not given a choice of boots and, in order to keep the price low, the cheapest boots of the poorest quality are often in the package. The bargain is not really a bargain. Go to another store and get the better boots.

I urge you to select your boots very carefully because they are so important.

## Skis

All right, you have your boots, which have determined what the rest of your equipment will be, so let's go on to skis.

There are three types of skis, and they are the same as that in boots: racing, mountaineering, and touring.

Racing skis, as you have probably already guessed, are extremely light in weight, not more than four pounds for the pair. They are narrow, usually measuring only about two and one-half inches wide at the most. Some wooden skis have edges made of hardwood or compressed hardwood, which is called lignostone. Skis made of fiberglass are definitely gaining in acceptance and popularity, primarily because they are light, strong, and require very little maintenance. The beautiful, hand-made wooden skis are becoming a thing of the past. There are some ski shops that still have them for sale, but most are leftovers. However, if you do happen to have a good pair of wooden skis, keep them because they are quite nice in many circumstances. Besides, who knows? They may come back into vogue.

At the other end of the ski spectrum are mountaineering skis, which come the closest to Alpine skis in appearance. Their width measures as much as three and three-eighths inches and they may weigh as much as eight pounds, which is very close to the ten-pound average weight of Alpine skis. Some mountaineering skis have full-length steel edges.

As with the boots, touring skis fall right in the middle of these two extremes. They usually weigh about six pounds for the pair and may be as wide as three inches, which is good for balance. Some touring skis have a three-foot metal edge, while others have full-length metal edges. (The latter type is more for mountaineering, however.) For timber bashing and powder snow touring, I recommend medium weight fiberglass touring skis.

There are many fine touring skis on the market today, so

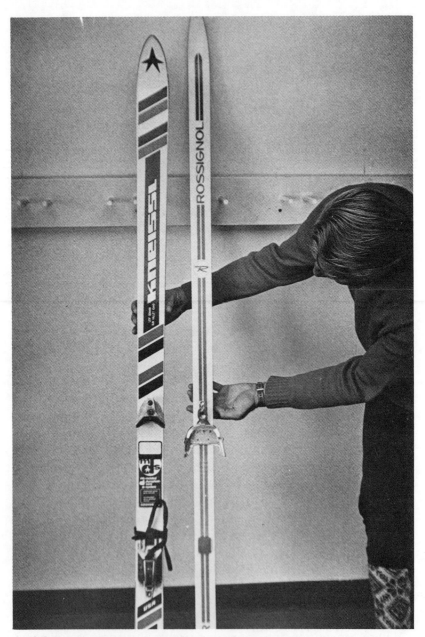

Leif Odmark examines the differences between alpine (left) and cross-country (right) skis. Besides the bindings, there is a difference in length, width, and weight.

pick out what appeals to you for the type of skiing you are going to do. When you make your selection, remember that the fit of the ski is important, although not as critical as in Alpine skiing. As a general rule, stand up straight and extend your arm straight above your head; the tip of the ski should just reach the palm of your hand. Another way to test for length is to stand up with your arm extended above your head, you should be able to curl your hand comfortably around the tip of the ski.

As I said, however, for cross-country ski touring, the length of the ski is not so important, so if you can't get a pair exactly the right length for you and the choice is between a ski that is too long and one that is too short, go to the one that better fits your weight. If you are slightly heavy, you will probably be more comfortable with a longer ski because of the additional carrying surface the extra length offers. If you are lighter in weight, the shorter pair will, most likely, suit you just fine.

The length of your cross-country skis is determined by your height and, sometimes, your weight. The skis should reach the palm of your upward-stretched hand. If you are on the heavy side, you will be happier in longer skis.

To wax or not to wax is a question that Nordic skiers are facing today, and it is a question that has no simple answer.

To wax or not to wax. The four skis on the left are fiberglass cross-country racing skis, the next one is a touring ski with plastic base, and the ski on the right has a wood base with lignostone edges.

Nonwax skis are an innovation that was introduced in about 1971 and met with almost instant acceptance. The basic principal of nonwax skis is relatively simple. They achieve their action by heat impressing a serrated grip-glide pattern on a polyethylene base, by inlaying fur strips in the base of the ski, by a step-pattern grip-glide implanted on the base, or by affixing replaceable prewaxed strips.

With all of these, there is some resistance to forward glide, which can and does reduce the ski kick-glide performance. Nonetheless, nonwax bases offer several advantages for recreational skiers, the biggest of which is they never need waxing. When skiing new wet or moist snow or wet spring snow, just rub some paraffin on the base of the waxless ski and into the groove and it works just great. (Be careful to avoid rubbing paraffin on the fur or the step-pattern.)

I strongly urge you to rent a pair of nonwax skis if at all possible before making a purchase. Try them out. They are excellent for beginners, and for those people who are willing to lose a little glide or who don't want to bother with waxing. Nonwax skis are definitely the easiest way to start, mostly because you have enough to learn in the beginning without having to bother to learn all about the different kinds of waxes as well. But of course, there is a world of difference between a nonwaxed ski and being on a well-waxed ski. There is no question but that the best running ski is the waxed ski. Waxing is something you may decide to go into later, if you do a lot of skiing or if you decide to become a purist.

If you are looking to buy nonwax skis, you will probably buy fiberglass with one of the artificial bottoms: mohair, fishscale, step-type and Swiss-type with replaceable strips. The step pattern is interesting to look at when you turn the skis over. You will see that the bottoms of these look like steps were cut in the area right under the foot. This, of course, prevents you from slipping backwards when you put your weight on the ski.

Waxed skis are a whole different ball game from nonwaxed skis. Many people are afraid to get into it, but you really

These are examples of waxless skis. The three on the left have step-patterns, the three on the right have mohair strips, and the one in the middle has a fishscale base.

shouldn't be frightened. Waxing can be challenging, fun, and rewarding.

Wax is a paste that, when correctly used, will stick to the snow when pressure is applied on the ski and will glide on the snow when the pressure is released. In other words, when you step down on your skis, you apply a pressure which causes the wax to grip or stick to the snow, then when you glide, the wax releases its grip.

If you don't apply the wax correctly, you are going to be in trouble—not danger, just unpleasant skiing. So I would encourage you to carefully follow the wax manufacturer's instructions.

Let me explain a little about the structure of snow and wax. First of all, they are both crystalline. The problem with snow is that it changes its structure with variations in temperature, pressure, and light. That basically explains why snow seems different in the shade than it does in the sunshine; why morning snow is different from noon snow; old from new; and the difference at varying altitudes. In addition, snow can be both viscous, or sticky, and elastic. Wax, on the other hand, is more stable, which is why we need a number of waxes for different snow conditions. Correct waxing, then, is applying the right wax in order to allow the right amount of glide for the snow condition.

How does the wax accomplish that? Remember I said both snow and wax are crystalline, so it is done through crystalline binding of the wax with the snow. If there is too much interlocking of wax and snow crystals, however, the wax is too soft and you will stick to the snow; but if the crystalline interlocking is very small or absent, then you will slip and not get enough grip. So it is important to make the correct choice.

The wax sticks to skis through the use and application of tar. Tar is used only on wood skis or those with wood bases and, in addition to giving the wax a means of staying on the ski, it also protects the ski against waterlogging. Tarring has to be done periodically when the white of the wood on the ski base begins to show. Materials used can range from drugstore pine tar to expensive preparations sold at a mountaineering shop. You also need a hand torch or a butane torch and some rags.

The procedure is fairly simple, and can be explained in four basic steps:

1. Clean off the old wax with a wax remover or a torch by heating carefully, then wiping. Repeat until the surface is clean.

2. Paint on the base compound—the pine tar or other tar preparation—with a brush or with rags.

3. Carefully torch the area until bubbles appear, but do not try to burn the tar in. Work on small areas, from six to eight inches of the ski, at a time.

4. Wipe with rags.

After a while, you will become so adept that you could almost do this procedure with your eyes closed, or at least while watching television.

As I have already mentioned, wooden skis are dying out, and there is reason for that. Fiberglass skis are very popular. With fiberglass, you don't have to worry about moisture or warping, and they are faster.

If you are using a fiberglass ski, instead of applying tar, you close the pores in the base by ironing on downhill paraffin wax. Then scrape off the excess, especially under the foot. Most new skis have an outline on the bottom to show you where to put the waxes and the kicker.

Now, before waxing for your tour, make a careful study of the immediate snow and weather conditions. Don't try to outguess Mother Nature and wax too far in advance. Wax, instead, at the starting point of your tour. It is, of course, ideal to know both the snow and air temperatures in order to determine any cooling or warming trends in the snow. In general, air temperatures alone are close enough indicators, but remember one thing: The warmest temperature snow can get is 32° F. If temperatures are below freezing, the snow is relatively dry; if air temperatures are above 32° F., you may have more or less wet snow conditions.

Some people carry thermometers along with them, but I would say that for the most part, thermometers are not very reliable for checking snow conditions because they are not actually in the snow. You stick one in the snow, of course, then take a reading, but you are really just getting the surface temperatures, which do not necessarily reflect the true snow conditions.

The best way to judge snow temperatures and conditions is to squeeze a handful of snow in the gloved hand. The glove, of course, is a protection against the possibility of getting a misreading based on body heat. So use a gloved hand, pick up a fistful of snow and squeeze. When you open your hand, you will have one of three types of snow: new or fine-grained snow with small, sharp crystals that puff away from your hand; coarse snow with large crystals that have developed after it has been on the ground a couple days; and crusty, or corn snow that develops from melting and refreezing.

You will soon learn to get a surprisingly accurate feel of the snow using this method. You won't be encumbered by having to carry a thermometer with you all of the time, in addition to having to wait for it to give you a reading.

If you are in doubt, always start with a harder wax—the colder the snow, the thinner and smoother the wax. If you have a hard wax as a base, you can always build softer layers on top of it. But if you start with a soft wax, you cannot possibly put a hard wax on top of a soft base. The whole thing will slip off. If you have a soft base on the skis and need a harder wax, you will have to scrape the ski bottoms and start over again. So always start with a harder wax for the glide, then work from there. And don't be lazy about smoothing out each layer you put on. Here are some general rules for applying wax:

1. Wax for the hardest conditions you expect.

2. Wax for the coldest conditions you think you will encounter.

3. In wet or spring snow, put a thin layer of paraffin on top of the skis to prevent icing.

4. Waterless soap will remove wax from your hands.

5. Ironing on wax gives the hardest surface; hand-smoothing gives the softest.

A cross-country skier takes time out on the trail to add a touch of wax to her skis. She is careful to rub the wax in and smooth it out with the aid of a cork.

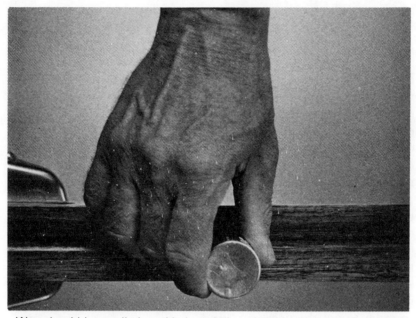

Wax should be applied to skis by rubbing. Put the surface wax directly on the ski, then rub it in using a cork.

After wax is applied to the base of the ski, smooth it out evenly by rubbing with a cork.

Another suggestion is to learn to wax by selecting and sticking to one brand. Knowing one brand of wax, its strong and weak points, speeds up your waxing time and you will have more time for touring. Experiment with the waxes, try different colors, and keep records. The same colors of waxes produced by different manufacturers don't necessarily do the same things, so don't confuse yourself by switching brands or mixing brands in the middle of the season.

A good thing to remember is the thicker the layer of wax, the better the grip; the thicker the layer, the less glide. So you can see if you put wax on, you should put on one thin coat, then work it very shiny. That's the glide. You will then want to adjust the kicker to continue the glide. Of course, if you know you have a tour coming that includes a lot of climbing, you will have to adjust to that fact and sacrifice a lot of glide in order to get the necessary kick.

## Bindings

You already have your boots, your skis, and you know about waxing. The next thing to consider is bindings. There are probably as many different bindings as there are snowflakes. Of course I am exaggerating, but there are a lot of different ones ranging from specialized to general to combination types. Again, the choice in bindings should heavily depend on use and the type of boots you will use. As a rule of thumb, as one's interests range from racing to mountaineering, the weight and complexity of the binding increases.

I would say that the three-pin, or mousetrap, bindings dominate the market. These are also known as the pole-operated bindings because they are made in such a way that you can clamp and undo them with your pole and you never even have to bend over.

As discussed earlier, most bindings and boot sole widths sold are called norm fit according to Nordic standards. The same binding size fits boot sizes ranging from a small lady's to a large man's.

However another type of binding, cable bindings, are excel-

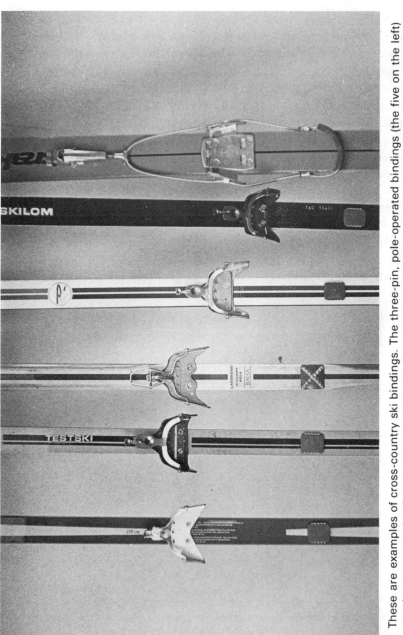

These are examples of cross-country ski bindings. The three-pin, pole-operated bindings (the five on the left) are the most popular for ski touring. Cable bindings (right) are excellent for ski mountaineers and for people who prefer mountain boots. The plates mounted at the heel on pin bindings are aids to help the skier keep his heel in place.

lent for people who ski occasionally in mountain-type or work boots and for ski mountaineering groups. Cable bindings come in various sizes, similar to old Alpine bindings, and have front toe and side hitches for downhill skiing. Many mountaineering bindings work as well as Alpine bindings, except that with the mountaineering bindings, the heel disengages to work up and down. This action is, of course, necessary for cross-country touring.

The important thing to remember about cable bindings is that they should be checked periodically for tightness.

### Poles

The last piece of equipment you will need for cross-country skiing is a pair of poles. As with the boots, skis, and bindings, the selection of the poles depends upon how you intend to ski. And, as with the other equipment, there is quite a variety

Ski tourers have a choice of materials when it comes to ski poles. From left to right are the tonkin or bamboo, aluminum, fiberglass/epoxy, and an alpine pole, which is used to illustrate the difference between downhill and cross-country poles. The alpine pole is thicker, sturdier, and more rigid, besides having finger grips on the handle.

from which to choose, including tonkin, aluminum, carbon fiber, and fiberglass. No matter which type you decide upon, look for general characteristics before you buy poles. They should be flexible, lively, and light to give an additional push.

Tonkin, which is another name for bamboo poles, used to be our tried and true standby, mostly because that is all there was. Today, however, tonkin poles are the cheapest to buy. The main problem with them is that, although they have the basic qualities of flexibility, liveliness, and lightness that we want in poles, they break very easily because they are very sensitive to temperature changes. For example, if you keep the tonkin inside where it is warm, then take it out skiing at about 10° F., you are likely to hear the pole snap as it cracks. You can tape tonkins, of course, and most people do to give them added strength. But despite this, if you lean on a tonkin pole, it can splinter.

In the past few years, some manufacturers have come out with aluminum poles that have the same good characteristics of the tonkin with the added advantage of combining lightness and liveliness with strength and durability. So, for general touring, I recommend that you buy high-quality aluminum poles. They will cost you a little more than the tonkin in the beginning, but they will be cheaper in the long run. Let me caution you against inexpensive aluminum poles. They are not a good buy.

If you are going to be racing, you will probably want extra lightweight aluminum, epoxy, or carbon fiber racing poles. The last two are also very good and acceptable for ski touring because they are very light in weight.

If you have been looking at cross-country ski poles, you have probably noticed that the tip—that part below the ring— is bent. That is not a defect in the pole, but rather a part of the design. It was made so that the pole extracts easily from the snow as you start to bring it forward. These tips take a lot of pressure, so you may also notice that racing poles have somewhat sturdier tips. Some racers go so far as to say that from 30 to 40 percent of the thrust they get in the diagonal

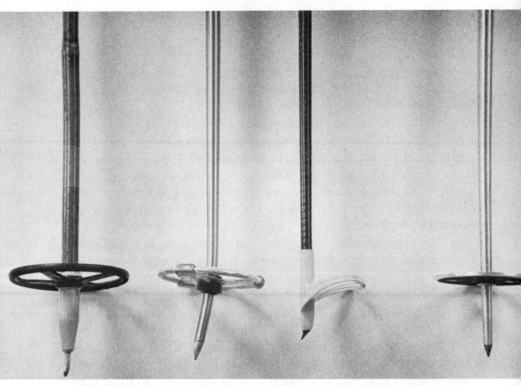

The tips (below the ring) of cross-country ski poles are bent forward to facilitate extraction from the snow as the skier starts to bring his pole forward. Can you pick out the alpine pole in the line above? It is the one on the right—the one with the straight tip.

stride comes from poling. For you, the ski tourer, it is just as important to get proper performance from your equipment, even though you may not be as concerned about speed as your racing counterpart.

In order to get proper performance from your poles, fit is important. The easiest way to test fit is to remember they should fit snugly under your armpit. That's not as strange as it may sound the first time you hear it. Measure your poles: Standing on the floor, stand your pole upright beside and slightly away from your body. Extend your arm straight out to the side at shoulder level, parallel to the ground. Rest your

When selecting poles, get a pair that fits snugly under the armpit. Buy the longer pole if you are between sizes. For all ski touring I recommend a high quality aluminum pole.

forearm on top of the pole. The pole should fit right there, snugly. If you are between sizes, take a longer pole. This may seem too long as you stand in the store, but remember that when you are skiing, the tip of the pole sinks down into the snow when it is planted.

## Clothing

Remember when you first started out, I suggested that you not buy special clothing for cross-country skiing, and that you ski in anything you happened to have in your closet. If you are serious about continuing ski touring, then you should be properly clothed. I am not talking about fashion, in this case, but style designed for the purposes of skiing. It really does make a difference.

Whatever you wear, be careful not to overdress. You do not want to perspire, but you do not want to be cold, either. The best solution is to wear layered clothing—thin layers of clothes that breathe. For example, when you go touring, you would be wearing a T-shirt, preferably of fishnet; a wool shirt, because wool remains a partial insulator, even if wet; and a windbreaker, such as a porous nylon shell with a hood that dries fast, or a down parka that is warm and also dries fast; or all of these. Depending upon the activity, these layers may be alternated in order to stay warm and dry.

Choose your man-made fabrics with care; be sure they breathe. If they don't, it could be like skiing in a steambath, and that is the surest way to get chilled and probably be laid up with a bad winter cold.

You will want to wear knickers for skiing because they provide freedom of the knees. Knee-movement is a high concern

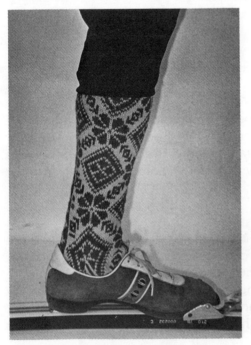

This is an example of a well turned-out low touring boot and pole-operated, three-pin binding. This skier is also wearing traditional knickers and kneesocks, giving him the flexibility of the knee that is essential to cross-country skiing.

in cross-country skiing. By and large, army fatigues and blue jeans are cold. Blue jeans also impair movement. Either wool, rayon, or poplin knickers are recommended. On a cold day, long johns are a must. Two pairs of knicker socks are recommended, and it is a good idea to bring a third pair.

Be sure to take along a hat, one that you can pull down to cover your ears.

Mittens rather than gloves are recommended for cross-country skiing. Your fingers can get too cold in tight Alpine-style gloves, but they stay warm and, by touching, keep each other warmer in mittens. There are some fine cross-country mittens on the market now that are light in weight yet warm and flexible. They have liners made of silk or wool that can be worn with or without the outer shell, which is usually made of leather. Again, the materials used are those that can breathe.

The rest of your equipment should match the type of skiing in which you intend to participate. Otherwise, the selection of proper clothing should follow common logic: Be warm but dry; and wear layered clothing to accomplish that goal.

## Care of Equipment

You have quite an investment in your equipment, so it will pay you to take good care of it. With the new synthetic materials that have replaced wood in skis, care is not quite as critical after each use. Just wipe the snow off the fiberglass skis and stand them in a corner, out of the way.

If you are using wooden skis, wipe them very carefully. Then stand the skis together and place a block about one and one-half to two inches thick right under the foot. Tie the skis together, tips and tails, with the block separating the two in the middle. The block is to keep camber, or bow, in the skis because, as you know, this is what gives you the grip.

The proper way to store wooden skis for the summer is to tie them together at the tips and at the tails, bottoms together. Then place a block under the foot to keep the camber.

Be sure that your bindings are wiped clean and dry for overnight as well as long-term storage. A touch of a lightweight oil, such as sewing machine oil, will keep all metal parts free of rust. There is almost nothing to do with the poles when you put them away, except to wipe them off.

The boots, too, should be dried thoroughly. Wipe off as much of the snow and water as possible, then stuff them with newspapers to keep their shape. If possible allow the boots to dry naturally. Don't put them on top of a heat source. Heat causes the leather to dry out and become brittle. When the leather is thoroughly dry, treat the boots with a good leather conditioner and waterproofer, such as mink oil or pure neat's-foot oil.

**For Children**

I would like to take a minute to mention children's equipment. For young children, the best and least expensive way to get started is exactly the opposite of what I recommend for adults. In this case, buy a small-sized package that includes skis, poles, and boots. You really don't have to worry about the quality of the boots for the youngsters, but do concern yourself with the fit.

Most of the children's packages include cable bindings, which are the best for kids because they provide more stability than the pin, or mousetrap, bindings. A typical ski designed for a child is built to the same standards as adult models and usually has premounted cable bindings with adjustable toe pieces to fit kids' boots. The poles in this small-sized equipment package are made with soft, plastic tips and enlarged wrist loops for safety.

So you can see that all the equipment for cross-country skiing is designed for comfort and safety for the whole family—from the small tots to the grandparents.

# 8
# The First Tour

You have been skiing around the backyard, through the neighborhood and across the golf course for a while now, and you are beginning to develop a rhythm and a stride. Cross-country skiing is fun, isn't it? If you agree, then you have gotten to the point where you are ready to go on your first tour.

Before you go, though, there are some things you should know and understand about touring on cross-country skis. Some of these are musts, and others are simply niceties.

Here I would like to mention the 5 Ps: Prior Planning Prevents Poor Performance. Think about that and you will be sure and plan well ahead of the tour.

The first thing is to determine where you are going to go. Select a destination. A good idea for the first tour is to choose a spot that, at any point along the route, you are no more than a half-mile from a major road or occupied home or lodge. Once you have more confidence and experience, and know the terrain better, then you may want to take longer trips.

Are you going to be gone for lunch? Remember, you are out to have a good time and to enjoy nature, so do not race or hurry. So it may be a good idea to take along a lunch. It is important always to take more food than you usually eat at home. This is because you burn up a lot more energy than you think, and you may be skiing longer than you expected. An extra sandwich, apple, or candy bar could prove invaluable in an emergency.

Next, check your equipment. Is it in good shape? Is it adequate? If you are using wax skis, is the base applied properly? Do you have the right color wax for today's conditions? Are you wearing warm socks? Are your pole straps adjusted to the right length? How about your clothing? Do you have enough layers to remove or to put on as weather conditions change? Do you have a hat? Gloves? Sunglasses?

Because you are probably going for lunch, you will be carrying a backpack or a fanny pack. There are some things that

Leif Odmark carries a well-equipped backpack on tours.

should go in it besides food. As routine, whether you are pic-
nicking or not, you should carry these things along when
touring: Windbreaker, gloves, extra wool socks, sunglasses,
avalanche cord, hat, emergency kit, and a wool sweater or a
down parka.

In addition, one person in your group should be designated
the leader, and should be outfitted with a pack that includes:
knife, screwdriver, pliers, steel wool (for fixing worn out screw
holes), touring binding parts (screws, wires, cables, thong),
windbreaker, wool sweater, cap, gloves, sunburn lotion, cork
and scraper, paraffin, water, first aid kit, and sunglasses.

Later on, as you do more touring and go on longer tours,
you will want to be prepared to efficiently and effectively handle emergencies in the wilderness. Therefore, you should make
yourself a kit that will provide the basic ingredients for

warmth, strength, and safety. The kit should be small enough as to not take up so much room that you wish you had left it behind, yet it should fulfill its purpose. You may even wish to consider assembling kits for each member of your party including children.

The items you should put in your emergency kit are:

1. Metal can, one pint size, with tightly sealing lid, for cooking.
2. Candle, for light and starting a fire.
3. Steel wool, for starting fires.
4. Matches.
5. Salt, to help overcome fatigue.
6. Bouillon cubes, for energy and nourishment.
7. Tea bags, to provide a hot drink as well as heat.
8. Space blanket, for signaling and heat.
9. Sealing tape, for patching.

Some of the other things that are always nice to have along are maps and a compass, flashlight, an assortment of waxes, an extra ski tip, aspirin, candy, nuts, and other snacks.

That may seem like an awful lot of superfluous equipment, but let me assure you that if you ever have to use any of these items, carrying them will certainly be worthwhile.

So now you may go off and enjoy yourself. Take it slow and easy; do not overdo your first time out, which is very easy to do. Often, the first tour is so exciting and so exhilarating that you suddenly find you have gone much too far.

If you are the first skiers in the area, don't forget to switch off breaking track. It is a good experience for each member to lead the group a little ways. If you are in an established cross-country ski area, where there are plenty of paths, tracks, and trails already, switching leads is not as important, but it is good experience nonetheless.

I will assure you of one thing—after touring today, spending the day in the fresh air, and enjoying nature's beauty—you will certainly sleep well tonight. Pleasant dreams!

# 9
# Competition

One phase of cross-country skiing that I have particularly enjoyed watching grow by leaps and bounds is what we call citizen races. I am not quite sure just what to attribute the tremendous growth in popularity to, whether it is television's influence in broadcasting Nordic events from the Olympics, or whether it is just man's natural instinct to be a highly competitive animal.

One type of competition is the President's Physical Fitness Program. In this program, you can receive your silver and gold pins and emblems. You get your own log book, which you can obtain from most ski touring centers—and I suggest that you keep your own log—and, after you have skied so many miles, you receive a very nice emblem or a pin.

Citizen races are an extremely popular form of competition. So, after you have started ski touring and moving around, you might like to become involved in a few citizen races. I am sure you will find that they really are a lot of fun. If you check around your area, I'm sure you will find that some group or organization sets up and sponsors this type of race.

More than 80 racers set off on a three-mile course in the first annual Reidy Memorial Cross Country Race at Sun Valley in March of 1972.

The citizen races are usually easy courses and there are usually classes for everyone—beginner men, beginner women, advanced, intermediate, expert, student, and seniors. With these categories, you are competing against people of your own sex, skiing ability, and age. The races are really a lot of fun and I would urge you to participate. Don't be afraid or embarrassed. Just get in there and sign up in your class.

Use the skis and other equipment you already have. Who cares if you have waxed or nonwaxed skis? Later, if you like racing, you may want to purchase some racing equipment. But to start, stick with what you have. It will be only the better racers, those in the top classes of citizen races, who will have special racing skis and poles.

Citizen races come in all sizes and varieties. In this one, Chris Nash gives JoAnne Levy a send-off in the second lap of a relay race. Their team won the Ladies' Division.

If you do decide to buy racing equipment, the first thing you will have to do is learn how to handle it. Today there are racing skis that are called fiberglass racers, and because of them, the sport has become a whole different ball game. Good fit is important, and racing skis should fit you in length and particularly camber.

As I mentioned in the chapter on equipment, fiberglass skis are made with more camber than wooden skis used to have. The amount of camber you need will be determined by your own weight and your own way of skiing. The individual's particular way of skiing in top racing differs from skier to skier. There is no set pattern, no right way, and no wrong way anymore. You will see someone bouncing a little more up and down, and you will see someone else bouncing a little less. Someone is more upright and someone else is more forward.

If you have ever seen Billy Cook, the American Olympian, race, you have seen that he has a great deal of camber and he bounces up and down more than anybody else. That is his style and, for him, it is the right one, although the same motion and style may not work at all for someone else. This explains why it is so important to develop your own pace, your own rhythm.

The greatest benefit in owning your own racing equipment is that it is lighter, and it is going to glide faster. If you can handle racing skis comfortably, you are going to go faster. It may take some time, though, so don't get discouraged. Instead, just put more and more miles on your skis.

It is a known fact that cross-country ski racing requires the highest level of physical fitness, according to studies made in Sweden in the late 1960s. In comparing aerobic capacity for men and women in several athletic events, doctors singled out cross-country ski racing as the number one. It exceeded distance running, cycling, swimming, and Alpine skiing, among other sports.

So conditioning is important. But don't back out of possibly racing by claiming that you are not in top physical condition. As you ski more and more and you like it, you will go out and tour once a week and maybe get out two or three times a week otherwise on the golf course or in your own backyard. In doing this, you naturally are going to get

Cross-country ski racers go at it.

stronger and stronger, and the skiing will become easier and easier. After the first race, you are likely to say, "Well, I did well, but I lost my wind a bit. I should be a little stronger." So you ski a little harder before the next race and, eventually, you will do better. Gradually you will become involved in more of a training program.

A lot of people, especially senior citizens, some of whom are 70 years old or more, become more involved in racing as they get older. So these citizen races are really a family sport because there are classes for everyone. Don't be afraid to get involved. Racing will help build up your skiing and your confidence, too.

The Grand Old Man of Skiing, centenarian Herman Smith-Johanssen, whisks across the finish of the "Jackrabbit Classic" at Sun Valley's 10th Annual Ski Club Reunion. "Jackrabbit" Johanssen, Reunion's guest of honor, is the best example of his own philosophy, "If you ski two miles a day you'll live to be a hundred."

# 10
# Potpourri

I have often been asked "Why should I go cross-country skiing? Why should I bother to learn?" Those are questions that have many, many different answers.

One answer might be, for example, that cross-country skiing is one way you can get out into nature during the winter. Your touring skis can carry you away from urban areas to explore creeks and follow meandering rivers. Skiing is an excellent way to exercise, as well as to share experiences with the whole family and with friends. Cross-country skiing is easy to do, so no one, be it a small child or a senior citizen, is excluded for lack of technical skills and potential danger.

There is a certain amount of freedom with cross-country skiing that you don't get from any other sport, including Alpine skiing. You don't have to wait in a lift line. You don't have to worry about turning. You don't have to fear that someone behind may run into you. Serious injuries, such as broken bones, are practically nonexistent in touring.

Cross-country skiing gives you a wonderful feeling of well-being. It is quiet. Your body is in good condition and you are relaxed, moving at your own pace, your own tempo. There is nothing to push you and no need to hurry.

There are, however, some things about cross-country skiing that you should definitely not do. For example, you must never ski alone, unless you are in an area such as a park or on a golf course where there is no danger of becoming lost. If you are skiing with a group of people, be sure someone in the group knows the area. If not, go into the Forest Service station or the park ranger's office and get a map of the area. And, while you are there, ask about areas that you should avoid for whatever reasons and ask about possible avalanche danger zones.

Do not overdo. Always, when you start off on a tour consider how strong the weakest member of your party is. No matter where you go and how far you travel, remember you always have to come back.

Always check your equipment before leaving to make sure it is in good condition and you haven't forgotten anything.

Always look at the weather and watch for warning signs of storms that might be coming. If you see evidence of bad weather, turn around and go back. Right now! Don't take chances. Be cautious. You are no match for Mother Nature.

This is a good place to talk about wind chill. Do not underestimate it. The wind chill is determined not only by the speed of the wind and the outside still-air temperature, but also the humidity. Even in the normally dry Rockies, if the temperature dips down to about 0° F., you could find humid conditions. Below zero the air dries up. A good rule of thumb is to deduct 3° F. times 10 percent of the humidity for temperatures above zero. For example, if you have a still-air temperature of 20° F. with a 10 mile per hour wind and 50 percent humidity, the effective temperature is -43° F.

When you are out, remember that snowmobiles, like cross-country skis, have their place. There is no question about that, and that is the way it should be: A place designated for the use of snowmobiles and a place designated for cross-country skiing. And never the twain shall meet. The two are totally incompatible. There is no way the two will ever coexist in the same area. Snowmobiles make too much noise to suit cross-country skiers who prefer the quiet as they glide along almost noiselessly, looking at wildlife, and do not want a noisy intrusion to spoil the peace they are enjoying.

In an area designated for touring, there are tracks made by other skiers. These trails get packed down after a while and become excellent for everyone on skis to use. Skiers really enjoy these tracks and like to have them, but a thoughtless snowmobile operator can wipe out the tracks and the skiers' pleasure with one swoop. And conversely, tracks made by snowmobiles are not good for cross-country skiing. They are too bumpy and do not give the skier a good glide.

So do yourself a big favor—stay out of snowmobile areas and hope snowmobilers stay out of yours.

Today it is a well-known fact that cross-country skiing is very much recommended by people in the medical profession. Doctors, themselves, say it is one of the best physical sports for the American people—old or young—who would normally be stuck indoors all winter long. The sport strengthens your muscles, keeps you limber, and increases your heart and lung capacity. And it is so inexpensive to do.

Another benefit of cross-country skiing is that it is the greatest calorie burner of all (see chart). Cross-country skiing burns far more calories than almost any other sport—walking, tennis, golf, whatever. Everything in your body, from head to toe, contributes something to cross-country ski movements.

You have learned enough to be comfortable on cross-country skis and can move around with a degree of ease. You can ski your golf course or you can go into a nearby forest and make a trial or follow an existing path. You can even ski on lakes or around lakes where it is truly beautiful. The ice, of course, should be thick and there should be a little snow, although you don't need much. Lake skiing is very much fun. You can see for miles and miles and aren't hampered by trees and hills.

Night skiing is something else you might enjoy, too. It is a very nice thing to do. If you have a full moon, you don't need

## The Urban Calorie Counter

| Activity | Calorie Expenditure Per Hour |
|---|---|
| Bicycle | 200–600 |
| Walk slowly | 115 |
| Walk moderately fast | 215 |
| Walk very fast | 565 |
| Football | 560 |
| Soccer | 560 |
| Rugby | 560 |
| Frisbee | 200 |
| Ball-throwing | 200 |
| Fly a kite | 30 |
| Take the family ice skating | 200–600 |
| A cross-country run through the park | 500–700 |
| Tackle an entire large museum in one day | 1,250 per day |
| Dance | 200–400 |
| Row energetically around a small lake | 500–900 |
| Roller-skate | 200–500 |
| Play basketball | 500 |
| Tennis | 500–700 |
| Cha-cha around the apartment | 200–500 |
| Skip rope | 300 |
| Take a horseback ride | |
|     Walking | 150 |
|     Trotting | 400–500 |
|     Galloping | 500–600 |
| Spend a lunch hour swimming at the "Y" | |
|     Breaststroke | 300–650 |
|     Backstroke | 300–650 |
|     Crawl | 300–700 |

| | |
|---|---|
| Judo | 800 |
| Exercise class | 250–820 |
| Skiing | |
|     Downhill running | 350–500 |
|     Cross-country | 650–1,000 |
| Volleyball | 300 |
| Weight lifting | 500 |
| Try cleaning your house yourself | |
|     Scrub floors (on your knees, with hands pushing out in front of you) | 165 |
|     Wash walls (stand a foot from the wall, holding a cloth in one hand and reaching as high as possible) | 165 |
|     Iron (with a 5-pound iron) | 50 |
|     Wash dishes | 50 |
|     Sweep (briskly) | 100 |
|     Paint your own apartment | 150–200 |
|     Scrape and sandpaper apartment walls | 180–250 |
|     Hang wallpaper | 150–200 |
|     Saw wood for your own bookcases | 300 |
|     Mow a friend's lawn | 300 |
|     At the next snow, shovel your own sidewalk | 5.4 to 12/minute |
| Golf (no cart allowed) | 133 |
| Keep most of your office and housekeeping materials on a high shelf and make yourself stretch and reach for them | 2.5/minute |
| Make your office phone calls standing up | 20 |
| Abandon elevators for stairs | 2.5/minute |
| Start every morning with a big s-t-r-e-t-c-h | 2.5/minute |
| Put on some John Philip Sousa music and march rapidly around the room | 550 |
| Card-playing | 100 |
| Billiards | 250 |
| Stand at cocktail parties | 20 |

any other light at all. Skiing by moonlight can be almost like skiing in daylight, so why not get a group together and take a tour at night. It is very enjoyable. If the moon doesn't happen to be big and bright, you can go ahead along the trail and light tiki torches or set candles in sand inside grocery sacks to outline the path. Or you can affix a headlamp to your ski cap, like a miner's lamp, and string the battery to your back pocket. You will be amazed at how well that type of light works.

If you really enjoy cross-country skiing, you will take every opportunity to do it. The more you ski, the better and stronger you will get.

If you have questions, you should always seek out a certified professional Nordic ski center, where you will get the right answers. Also talk to Forest Service Station personnel, who are becoming more involved in Nordic skiing.

We who live in Sun Valley and those who come to the Sun Valley Nordic Ski School have a very big advantage in planning tours. For example, we often take a day trip to a warm springs area where we refresh ourselves in a natural hot spring before returning to the Nordic Center.

We take buses to starting points for day tours and overnighters during which we follow such creeks as Prairie, Cherry, Senate and Wild Horse. Our tours take us to interesting areas such as North Fork, Western Holme, and Emma Gulch. There are literally hundreds of uninhabited and unspoiled valleys to the north of Sun Valley, and we have seen most of them on cross-country skis. For the most part, these places are inaccessible by any other means of transportation. Most of the land is within the Sawtooth National Forest and is protected against use by snowmobiles. They are usually sent to their own designated area a few miles farther on. This makes everyone—skier and snowmobiler alike—very happy. We peacefully coexist, neither one infringing on the other's territory.

We have a helicopter service at the Sun Valley Nordic Ski School which we use often and enjoy tremendously. We fly out, have lunch, then ski back to the Nordic Center; or we do

Helicopter cross-country skiers are dropped in virgin country.

it the other way around. We sometimes fly to previously un-tracked spots miles and miles from the closest highways. I wish I could describe the beautiful sight that comes from looking down on Trail Creek Summit then landing in Copper Basin in the shadow of Devil's Bedstead Mountain, where a herd of antelope is usually at play. Here we can ski powder snow all day, see a variety of other wildlife, and an assortment of nature's beauty before we fly back home. Helicopter skiing is an exciting adventure in cross-country skiing that is going to greatly increase in popularity.

So as you can see, the potential for cross-country skiing is unlimited. Just go at it and enjoy yourself. But do join me in this pledge:

### Ski Tourer's Pledge

I will protect the land and natural resources of the land on which I ski. I will make it my personal business to leave the land in such a condition that, except for the tracks of my skis upon the snow, no one will ever know that I was there. I will always treat the land gently so that I may return in the future and be welcomed as an old friend.

# Index

**U**

U.S. Olympic cross-country team, vi, *illus.* 8
Uphill, 43-50, *illus.* 43, 44
  diagonal stride, 44
  herringbone, 47-50, *illus.* 48
  picking up skis, 44-45, *illus.* 45
  side-stepping forward, 47, *illus.* 47
  side-stepping upward, 45-47, *illus.* 46
  tacking, 49-50, *illus.* 49

**V**

Vasaloppet, 3-4

**W**

Walking, 7
Waxed skis. *See* Skis
Waxing, 89-94, *illus.* 92, 93
Weather conditions, 114
Wedge. *See* Snowplow
Weight distribution, 32, 50, 53, 57, 64, 66. *See also* Forward lean
Weight transfer, 35-36
Wind chill, 114
Wooden skis. *See* Skis

**Y**

YMCA, 7